GAIL BROWN'S ALL-NEW

INSTANT INTERIORS

DECORATE WITH FABRIC, *FAST*

About the Author

Gail Brown ranks as one of the industry's most widely read sewing journalists, recognized for her innovative methods and writing style. Her work has appeared in *McCall's Pattern Magazine*, *Sew News*, *The Singer Sewing Library*, *Woman's Day Home Decorating Ideas*, and *Vogue Patterns Magazine*, and she is a frequent guest on Nancy Zieman's "Sewing with Nancy" PBS television show. Gail is also a columnist and consulting editor for the *Update* newsletters, and has been an instructor for the Palmer/Pletsch Serger Workshops.

Although this home-economics graduate started her career 20 years ago in New York City, she now transmits via modem and facsimile from the small coastal town of Hoquiam, Washington. Her patient husband, John Quigg, and two children, Bett and Jack, share her home/office, putting up with her deadline-panic attacks, and growing collection of fabrics, sergers, sewing machines, needlework collectibles, and Macintosh-computer paraphernalia. Currently concentrating on articles and copywriting, Gail is contemplating her next book project, and attempting to work

less. Don't hesitate to send her your questions, comments, and suggestions—write Gail
c/o Open Chain Publishing,
P.O. Box 2634-BK,
Menlo Park, CA 94026.

Other Books by the Author

Quick Napkin Creations
  (*Quick Napkin Creations* video, with Nancy Zieman, also available)

Innovative Sewing
  (with Tammy Young)

Innovative Serging
  (with Tammy Young)

Creative Serging Illustrated
  (with Sue Green and Pati Palmer)

Creative Serging
  (with Sue Green and Pati Palmer)

Sewing with Sergers
  (with Pati Palmer)

Sensational Silk

Sew A Beautiful Wedding
  (with Karen Dillon)

Super Sweater Idea Book
  (with Gail Hamilton)

GAIL BROWN'S ALL-NEW

INSTANT INTERIORS

DECORATE WITH FABRIC, *FAST*

"My test for a sewing book is this: Does it make me want to head straight for my sewing machine? Gail has taken such an easy, spontaneous, and joyful approach to decorator sewing that I felt like threading the machine by the time I finished reading Chapter One. Gail knows how to keep it all clear, concise, and complete. This is the kind of sewing book which will encourage your creativity."

Peggy Bendel, Contributing Editor, Sew News

"Mindboggling—it's the only word for this compact, comprehensive home-dec book. Gail's eliminated the frustration of yardage estimates and calculations. You just buy the fabric, sew it, and enjoy it—tonight!"

Clotilde, President, Clotilde, Inc.

"Decorating with fabric is incredibly popular, perfect for sewers and non-sewers alike. And Gail Brown has made decorating with fabric easier, faster, and more fun than ever."

Gail Hamilton, Vice-President, Advertising & Promotional Services, McCall Pattern Company

"Wow! These are Gail's best ideas yet. Gail deserves a big hand for giving so much to home sewers. Each of her books is a treasure to anyone's creative library and **Instant Interiors** is no exception."

Joanne Ross, Program Chair, Sewing and Stitchery Expo, Washington State University

"Whether you sew or not, you'll love this book for decorating inspiration—from quick how-to's, yardage charts and tips, to great-looking home fashions simply not found in another book or pattern."

Jan Saunders, Author, **Teach Yourself to Sew Better** series

"This book is a refreshing new approach in decorating how-to books. Its emphasis on **quick** and **easy** makes decorating fun for everyone. The Quick Yardage Calculation charts are worth the price of the book alone."

Sharon Stoffel, Executive Vice President/General Manager, Pacific Fabrics

"Gail Brown has done it again with this wonderful potpourri of budget-wise and beautiful decorating ideas. Anyone can create these designer looks in no time, using Gail's super sewing shortcuts and no-sew strategies!

Barbara Weiland, Managing Editor, That Patchwork Place

"Gail Brown's book is the first sewing/decorating book that I've read that was written and designed in 'cookbook' format—each page has a decorating idea with concise instructions. You don't have to read through pages of basic sewing instructions to get to the heart of Gail's great ideas; like a cookbook, the 'white sauce' information is in the back."

Nancy Zieman, National TV Hostess, "Sewing With Nancy"

CHILTON BOOK COMPANY
Radnor, Pennsylvania

Acknowledgments

One of my six brothers-in-law, Patrick Quigg, told me that my book acknowledgments remind him of too-long Academy-Award acceptance speeches. So, in an effort to succinctly recognize those many people and companies who help me put together a book project, I will list them. Although this format is rather impersonal, my appreciation is no less personal and heartfelt. *Thank you:*

• Bobbie Keeney, dear friend and publisher of the *Instant Interiors* booklets, for giving me and Open Chain Publishing the opportunity to work with her material.

• John, Bett, Jack, and the rest of my family for hardly ever complaining (well, sometimes...) about my endless cancellations, postponements, and absences "because the book isn't done yet." (I am looking forward to being a more normal wife and mother, although my daughter says I "will never be normal, so don't try.")

• Robbie Fanning (the industry's best editor), Cate Keller, Rosalie Cooke, and the entire Open Chain staff, for tolerating my serial deadline extensions. Also, for their expertise, persistence, intelligence, unflagging sense of humor, and shared passion for machines—sewing, serger, Macintoshes, modems, facsimiles, and other electronic goodies.

• Linda Wisner, my former partner, and coauthor/designer of *Creative Serging for the Home* (Palmer/Pletsch), for collaborating with Bobbie Keeney and me to develop the first *Instant Interiors* publications.

• Naomi Baker, fellow free-lancer, bestselling author, and seamstress-who-has-no-equal, for talking me out of getting a "real job" when my writing world goes temporarily berserk.

• Susan Foster and Pati Palmer, for giving me a start, and for sharing their valuable insights.

• Donna Cook, who does everything else so that I can work, and not be crazed about everything else when I'm not working.

• Father Dave Rogerson, head of my computer-maintenance crew (of one) for being a friend who regularly asks, "How can I help?"

• Bernina, Brother International, Elna, Juki of America, Kenmore, Necchi, New Home, Pantograms, Omnistitch, Pfaff, Singer, Tacony, Toyota, Viking, and White for generously providing the latest machines and information.

• Participating fabric and trim companies—Concord House, Fabric Traditions, Hollywood Trims, and V.I.P. Fabrics—for their feedback and product contributions—see page 92.

• Notion distributors and manufacturers for explaining and supplying their newest time-saving tools—see pages 92 and 93 – 95.

• Sewing professionals Clotilde, Dianne Giancola, Mary Giese, Jan Healzer, Nel Howard, Janet Klaer, Adele Martinek, Betty Quinell, Jane Schenck, Ann Thomassen, Victoria Waller, and Nancy Zieman for finding time in their incredibly busy schedules to comment on my pre-publication drafts.

• Bracey Plaeger, Roz Carson, Heather McLaren, Lee Lindeman, Elaine Acosta, and Virginia Fulcher, the illustrator, designers, photographer, and samplemakers who expand and enhance my visions.

For this necessarily long list, my apologies to Patrick.

Copyright © 1992 Gail Brown

All rights reserved.

Published in Radnor, Pennsylvania 19089, by Chilton Book Company

ISBN 0-932086-33-0

Library of Congress Catalog Card Number 92-060757

Color photographs by Lee Lindeman

Interior design by Gail Brown and Heather McLaren

Cover design and interior color placement by Rosalyn Carson

Illustrations by Bracey Plaeger

Printed in the USA

Contents

Welcome to Instant, Elegant Interiors

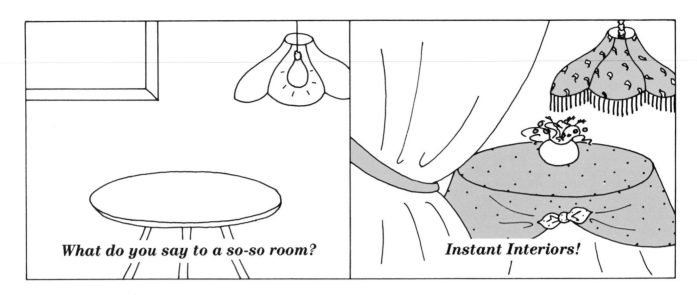

What do you say to a so-so room?

Instant Interiors!

At a recent seminar, one of my students announced, *"Thank you. You've granted me the freedom to take decorating shortcuts—fuse-finishing edges, rubber-banding hems, tying on pillow covers— without feeling guilty or shortchanged."*

After you read just one page of this book, I hope you share those sentiments. For me, shortcuts are a necessity. With a more-than-full-time job, a family, church, community commitments and more, I simply don't have time for tedious projects. And I don't have the inclination or budget to buy inferior ready-mades or spendy custom services. Yet, like you, I crave creative, and yes, even elegant, living and working environments.

The answer to my decorating dilemma? *Fabric and lots of it.* With minimal carpentry skills, I can "paint" my walls and valance my windows. With no upholstery skills whatsoever, I can slipcover a chair or sofa. With only an hour of free time, I can make a table topper or curtain a shower. Professional-looking projects result from clever construction strategies and lavish use of fabric. You too can discover the practical magic of decorating with fabric, *fast.* Here's how:

• *Dive into this book—and decorating—wherever you'd prefer.* Look over the "Contents"—see page 5. Project how-to's are all one-page, start to finish, and include "The Materials" and "The Steps." You'll also find "idea pages"—easy variations and additional quick projects.

• *If you're under a time crunch, haven't sewn in a long time, or are just learning to sew,* start with one of the easiest projects, such as "Napkins & Rings in No Time"—see page 14, "Wow! Pillows in an Instant!"—see page 50, or "Hurried Holiday Transformations"—see page 66. Notice that the last page of each chapter features some of the fastest-to-make project ideas. Build your confidence, then move to a larger or more involved project—don't worry, all techniques in this book are some degree of fast.

• *Look up background information*—yardages, techniques, products—in the "Instant Interiors' Time-, Money- and Sanity-Saving Guide"—see pages 67 – 96.

• *Having difficulty finding the right fabrics, notions and hardware?* After exhausting all local possibilities, consult the "Sources"—see pages 93 – 95.

• *Temporarily lost a project or technique?* Skim the "Index" where all subjects are alphabetized—see page 96.

Enjoy *Instant Interiors*—the fun, the fabrics, the lovely furnishings.

Camouflage Storage

Showcase Cherished Tables

1

TIMESAVING
TABLE TOPPERS

Dress-Up Everyday Dining

Create Affordable Furniture

Simple, Classic Squares & Rectangles

Think of square or rectangular cloths as over-sized napkins draped over your tables. Sound easy to make? They are.

The Materials

• **Fabric:** Just about any fabric type or weight. You'll need 3-1/4 yards of 36" – 54" widths for a 34"-diameter cloth with a 10"-drop (3 meters of 90cm – 140cm widths for an 86cm-diameter cloth with a 25cm-drop).

The Steps

1. Cut the necessary number of lengths from the total yardage required—see pages 82 – 83.

2. Piece to avoid a seam running down the center of the table—see page 71. Trim to the desired unfinished dimensions, allowing 1-1/2" (4cm) hem allowances on all sides—only 1/4" (6mm) if serge-finishing.

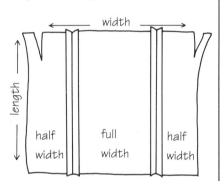

3. Hem or finish the edges. For uniform corners, work opposite side to side. All hemming and finishing how-to's are on pages 72 – 73.

• **No-sew:** Fuse (see "Fast-fused" hems and "Fast-folded-and-fused" miters).

• **Easy-sew:** *For fastest miters,* follow the "Fast-folded-and-stitched" miters. *For stitched miters,* follow the "Easy-sew miter" technique. For a stable,

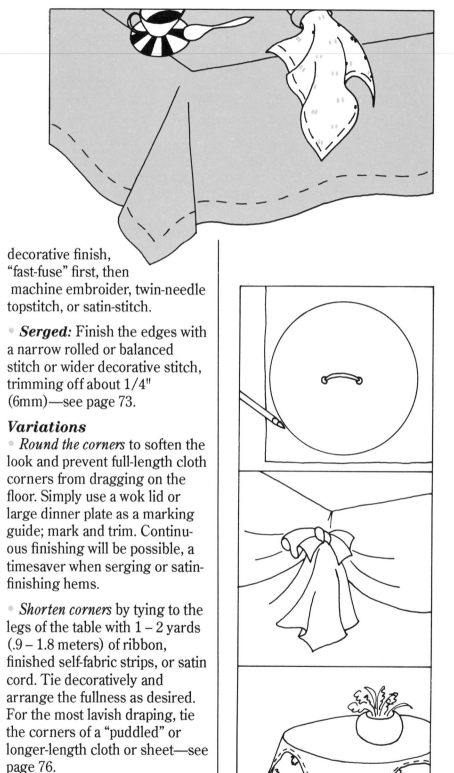

decorative finish, "fast-fuse" first, then machine embroider, twin-needle topstitch, or satin-stitch.

• **Serged:** Finish the edges with a narrow rolled or balanced stitch or wider decorative stitch, trimming off about 1/4" (6mm)—see page 73.

Variations

• *Round the corners* to soften the look and prevent full-length cloth corners from dragging on the floor. Simply use a wok lid or large dinner plate as a marking guide; mark and trim. Continuous finishing will be possible, a timesaver when serging or satin-finishing hems.

• *Shorten corners* by tying to the legs of the table with 1 – 2 yards (.9 – 1.8 meters) of ribbon, finished self-fabric strips, or satin cord. Tie decoratively and arrange the fullness as desired. For the most lavish draping, tie the corners of a "puddled" or longer-length cloth or sheet—see page 76.

• *Make a versatile square "topper"* for any square or round table. For yardages, see page 83. Hem or finish, and use as is or over a longer cloth.

Really Easy Round Tablecloths

Round tablecloths . . . there's not a more versatile decorator accessory. A "clothed" round can be a dining or end table, a bed or lamp stand, or a clever storage cover-up. No round table? Buy an inexpensive particle-board table or top from your nearest fabric or discount store or a mail-order catalog, then cover with fabric.

The Materials
• **Fabric:** Just about any type or weight. You'll need 5 yards of 45" – 72" widths for a full-length, 30"-diameter cloth (4.6 meters of 115cm – 180cm widths for a full-length 76cm-diameter cloth).

The Steps
1. Cut the necessary number of lengths from the total yardage required—see pages 82 – 83.

2. Piece as described in Step 2 on page 8. Allow only 1" for hems— 3/4" (2cm) if fusing, or 1/4" (6mm) if serge finishing. Narrow allowances will require less easing at the hemline edge.

3. Round the cloth for hemming, as shown on page 71. Quarter-fold, aligning the piecing seams. Pin a measuring tape to the center point of the fold. Mark half the unhemmed length on the tape. Pivot the tape, mark a quarter-circle, and trim along the markings through all four layers. *Optional:* Some seamsters find it more accurate to half-fold the pieced cloth and then round.

4. Hem or finish the edge. All hemming and finishing how-to's are on pages 72 – 73.

• **No-sew:** Finish with "Fast-fused edges"—see page 73. The inside edge of the transfer-web tape will require intermittent lapping, as it curves to fit the larger outer edge.

• **Easy-sew:** If ravel-prone, finish the edge with pinking, zigzagging, or serging. Turn up the hem; pressing is optional but often unnecessary. From the right side, topstitch about 1/2" (1.3cm) from the hemline.

• **Serged:** Finish the edges as described for "Serged Round Napkins," on page 14. *Optional:* Serge-finish with decorative thread, and a wider, balanced stitch—see page 73.

No-more-edge-stretching tips: Ease-plus the fabric, force-feeding it into the foot while holding the fabric against the back of the foot. Or use differential feed to ease-plus; set on 1.5 – 2, if your serger has this handy feature.

Variation
• *Swag the edge of any round topper.* When calculating the cloth size, double the drop length—see page 83. Hem the edge. Cut six pieces of shirring tape the length of the finished drop. If using sew-on tapes, add 1" (2.5cm) for turning under 1/2" (1.3cm) at both ends—see page 18. Evenly space the tape on the wrong side, then fuse or stitch in place. Shirr

Swag with shirring tape.

Terrific Table-Top Variations

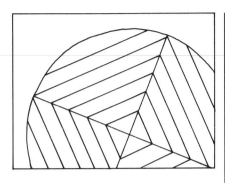

• **Chevron stripes or borders.**
The fabric width must be equal to
or greater than half the
unhemmed tablecloth width.

1. Draw the pattern as shown.
Using the pattern, cut out four
identical triangles of fabric.

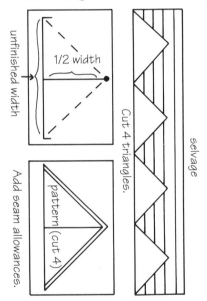

unfinished width

1/2 width

Add seam allowances.

pattern (cut 4)

Cut 4 triangles.

selvage

2. Seam the triangles together in
pairs, then seam the pairs
together. Hem. *Optional:* Trim to
a round—see page 71.

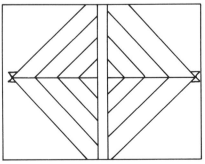

Seam triangles in pairs.

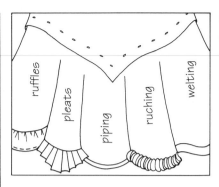

ruffles

pleats

piping

ruching

welting

• **Accent, weight, or lengthen**
any cloth with ruffles, pleats,
piping, ruching, or welting—see
pages 74 – 75.

• **Swag without sewing.**
Loosely knot the corners,
tucking in the tails. Or with
rubber bands, secure ascots or
rosettes at each corner (or
quarter-mark). The longer the
cloth, the larger the knots,
ascots, or rosettes, and the
deeper the swags. *Variation:* Pull
poufs through small plastic or
brass rings, or rosettes through
swag holders, such as *Infinity
Rings* from Repcon—see page 80.

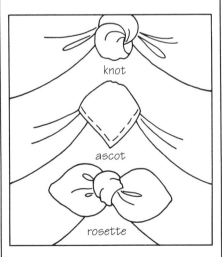

knot

ascot

rosette

• **"Puddle" a cloth** by simply
tucking under a wide 20"
(51cm)+ allowance at hem edges.
Hem finishing is optional—see
page 76.

• **Skirt your table without
sewing.** Start with a round, oval,
or vanity utility table. Cut the
fabric 2.5 times the top
circumference by its full width.
Fabric should be at least 45"
(115cm) wide. Quarter-mark one
selvage and the table edge.
Match the marks and staple,
lapping the skirt selvage edges
over the table edge; the hem can
be straight or puddled. Push-pin
to pleat the fabric evenly. Then
staple the pleats, camouflaging
the opening. Remove push pins.
Cover with a topper—see page 8.

Staple pleats.

Cover with a topper.

• **Buffer and protect tables.**
Cut a fleece layer the top size.

• **Soil-proof and showcase,**
by covering the fabriced table top
with custom-cut 1/4"(6mm)
glass. A photo or art gallery can
be displayed underneath, too.

• **Cloth too long when the
table leaves are removed?**
Shorten, instantly, by softly box-
pleating the center section.

Ovals & Vanities: Clever Coverings

Ever been frustrated when shopping for a cloth to cover an oval table? If so, opt for the easy, custom-fit alternative: Make your own, fast.

The Materials

• **Fabric:** Any tightly woven light- to mid-weight. For a 40"-wide by 60"-long cloth with a 10" drop, you'll need 4-1/2 yards of 45"- to 60"-wide fabric. (For a 102cm-wide by 150cm-long cloth with a 25cm drop, you'll need 4.2 meters of 115cm- to 150cm-wide fabric.)

The Steps for Ovals

1. Cut the necessary number of lengths from the total yardage required—see pages 82 – 83.

2. Piece to avoid a seam running down the center of the table—see page 71. Center the pieced cloth right side down on the table, holding in place with weights, like soup cans.

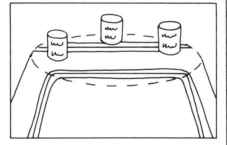

3. Using tailor's chalk or erasable fabric marker, trace the edge of the table on the wrong side of the cloth.

4. Take the cloth off the table and lay flat. Measure and mark the desired drop plus a 1" hem— 1/4" if serge finishing—from the table-edge marking. Trim to the hemline.

5. Hem or finish the edge using one of the methods described in Step 4 on page 9.

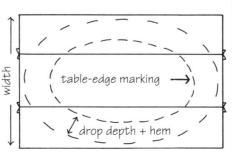

width

table-edge marking →

drop depth + hem

Skirted Vanity Variation

1. Trace the edge of the table on butcher-paper or newsprint. Add a 1/2" (1.3cm) seam allowance. Using the pattern, cut out one piece of fabric and if desired for additional body, one piece of fusible fleece fused to the *wrong side* of the fabric.

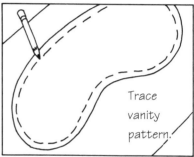

Trace vanity pattern.

2. Skirt the top with a rectangle that measures 2 to 2-1/2 times the top circumference by the vanity height plus 4-1/2" (11.4cm). Seam into a circle, then fuse or stitch a 2" (5cm) double hem—see pages 71 – 72. Gather the opposite edge, and seam to the top with a 1/2" (1.3cm) allowance, right sides together.

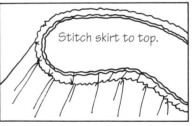

Stitch skirt to top.

Optional: Make a matching stool cover. Consider protecting the vanity with a glass top, cut from the same pattern without seams.

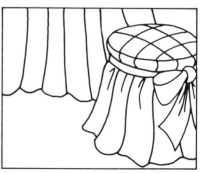

Practical Pizzazz: Placemats

● **Quickly convert napkins into mats.** Position diagonally under the plate, letting a point hang over the table edge. Or fold a large 24" (61cm)-square napkin or any edge-finished fabric square into a clever, quick mat—see below. *Variation:* If lined, the corners can be tucked under, rather than folded back.

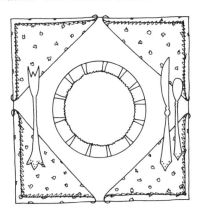

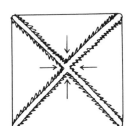

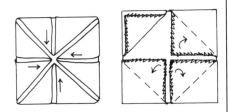

● **Cut out mats (no-sewing!) from any ravel-free vinyl.** Trim to the size and shape desired, or follow the free-form outline of the print motif.

● **Miter rectangular mats, fast.** Cut out 16" by 21" (41cm by 53cm) rectangles. Finish all the edges, trimming or folding under about 1/4" (6mm) with pinking, satin-stitching, hemming, or serging. Press up

the two shorter sides 1-1/4" (2.5cm) *to the right or wrong side.* Repeat for the remaining opposite sides, folding to form corner miters. Topstitch 1" (2.5cm) from the edge.

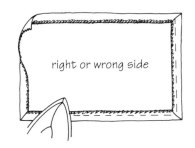

right or wrong side

Optional: Insert fusible web tape under the miter fold; fuse. *No-sew variation:* See "Fast-folded-and-fused," miters, page 73.

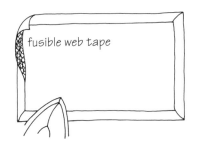

fusible web tape

Satin-stitched variation: Don't edge-finish first; press the hems, and then satin stitch over the raw edges.

satin stitch

Goof-proof-fabric tip: Stick with heavier fabrics for mats, or beef up lighter-weights—see page 70.

Bordered variation: Cut a 12" by 17" (30cm by 43cm) insert from contrasting fabric, which you may want to quilt or pleat before cutting out—see page 70. After

pressing the hems, center the insert inside the hems, *wrong sides* together. Stitch the edges down, through all layers, securing the insert.

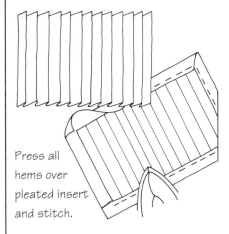

Press all hems over pleated insert and stitch.

● **Easily edge-finish oval mats.** Use a purchased mat as a pattern, or round the corners of a 13" by 18" (33cm by 44cm) rectangle. Start edge-finishing at the center of one of the longer edges; the joining can be hidden under the plate. For binding and serge-finishing options, see pages 74 – 75.

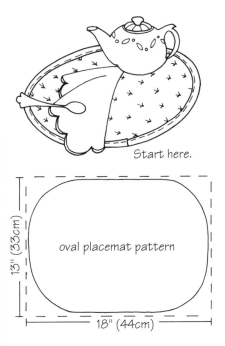

Start here.

13" (33cm)

oval placemat pattern

18" (44cm)

Instant Elegance: Runners

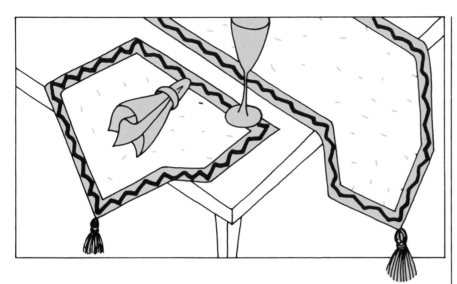

Runners require less fabric than other covers, and show off the finest tables. Crisscross on a table and they double as placemats.

The Materials
- *Fabric:* Any mid-weight or heavier. *Width guidelines:* From 12" (30cm) to 20" (51cm) if used as a placemat, plus 3" (7.5cm) for two 1-1/2" (4cm) hem allowances. If binding, do not add allowances. *Length guidelines:* As needed—although drops of at least 12" (30.5cm) hang more luxuriously—plus 3" (7.5cm) for two 1-1/2" (4cm) hem allowances. *If the runner is not pieced,* its length will be the yardage required. Also, see page 83.

The Steps
1. Cut out the fabric on either the lengthwise or crosswise grain, whichever minimizes piecing.

2. Piece to achieve the length desired. Center the piecing seam.

3. Fuse or stitch a double-hem: 3/4" (2cm) in the short ends first, then in the longer sides. Or bind or serge-finish the edges—see pages 74.

Variations
- Weight straight runner ends with a 1/2" (1.3cm) dowel. Allow for and stitch 1" (2.5cm) casings in the short ends; insert the dowels.

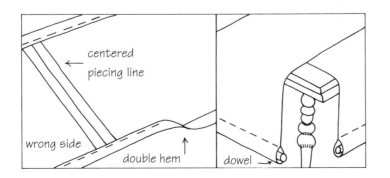

- *Chevron the runner ends.* Hem or finish the longer sides first. Then fold one end right sides together, and seam with a 3/8" (1mm) allowance. Press the seam, turn right side out, and press again. Repeat for the other end. *Optional:* Topstitch or accent with trim and tassels.

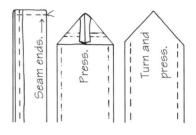

- *Self-line a runner.* Cut the runner twice the finished width plus 1" (2.5cm) by the length desired plus 1" (2.5cm). Fold the runner in half, lengthwise, right sides together; stitch with a 1/2" (1.3cm) seam allowance, centering a 6" (15cm) opening in the seam. Press the seam open. Before turning right side out, stitch the ends—either straight across or press-mark the chevron lines (fold as shown above), stitch, and trim. Turn through the opening and press.

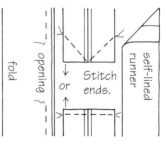

- *Make runner placemats* with one straight and one chevroned end—see drawing below. Finish to about 18" (46cm) wide by 20" (57cm) long. Combine with a full-length runner—elegant!

Napkins & Rings in No Time

- **No-sew: Finish napkins with "Fast-fused" edges**—see page 73. Use 3/4" (2cm)-wide fusible-transfer web strips. The unsewn, fused edges are amazingly durable. Or use this finish as a palette for machine stitchery; the stable fused edges prevent tunneling. *Variation:* Fold miters before fusing the last two sides.

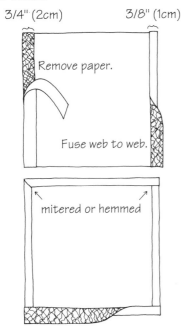

3/4" (2cm)   3/8" (1cm)

Remove paper.

Fuse web to web.

mitered or hemmed

- **Easy-sew: Fold a mitered edge, fast.** Finish all the edges with pinking, serging, zig-zagging, or a 1/4" (6mm) hem. Press 1" (2.5cm) hems, folding corner miters. Topstitch the hem and miters about 3/4" (2cm) from the hemline folds.

right or wrong side

- **Serged: Continuously edge-finish round napkins.** To cut out, use a 20" (51cm) or larger template, such as a large wok lid or a cardboard or acrylic round drawn by rotating a measuring tape. Sheets of acrylic are available in art or quilting stores. Serge-finish the edges, starting and finishing in the 1-1/4" (3cm)-long by 1/4" (6mm)-deep notch cut in the edge. *Variation:* Round off a square napkin, and serge-finish in the same manner. I prefer starting with 20" (51cm) squares (smaller squares can look skimpy after rounding).

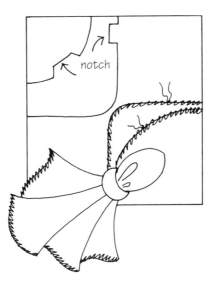

notch

- **Tie napkin rings out of wired-edge ribbons**—see pages 58 – 59. To shape the opening, form around an empty paper towel or tissue roll.

- **Tassel a cord** (thanks, Victoria Waller). Tape the end of a cord and slip it through a tassel loop; pull down on the loop, and push the cord into the tassel end with a scissors point. Add a drop of glue. Repeat for the other cord end. Wrap the napkin as shown.

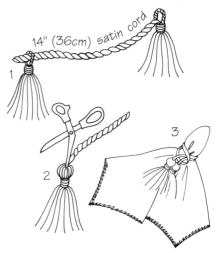

14" (36cm) satin cord

1

2   3

- **Transform a napkin into a matching ring.** Fold in corners and pull through a 1" (2.5cm) *Infinity Ring*—see page 80—or small plastic or brass ring.

small ring

Infinity Ring

For extensive napkin and napkin-ring how-to's, refer to my *Quick Napkin Creations* book—see page 92.

Soften a Frame or View

Divide a Room, or Curtain a Doorway

2

QUICKEST CURTAINS

Visually Alter the Window Size

Add Accent & Privacy

Quick! Shirred Curtains

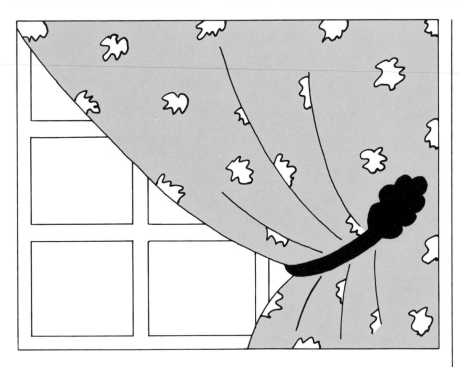

Shirred curtains are incredibly versatile. No matter what the style of your home, shirrs can enhance the look without being overly frou-frou. Plus, they effectively soften the horizontal lines synonymous with popular mini-blinds and woven woods.

The Materials

- **Fabric:** Any light- to mid-weight cotton. You will need 3-1/3 yards of 45"-wide fabric or one twin sheet for a finished curtain 62" wide by 38" long. This will cover a window or area 31" wide by 38" long in a 2:1 ratio. (You will need 3 meters of 115cm-wide fabric or one twin sheet for a finished curtain 155cm wide by 95cm long. This will cover a window or area 77cm wide by 95cm long in a 2:1 ratio). For custom calculations and other yardages, see pages 84 – 85.

- **Hardware:** Any rod adjustable to or cut to the desired width—see page 80.

- **Optional:** *Light- to mid-weight lining*—yardage requirements are the same as for the fabric. Also tiebacks—see page 17.

The Steps

1. Cut the necessary number of lengths from the total yardage—see pages 84 – 85.

2. Piece to avoid a seam running down the center of the curtain. You can trim to the total width required, although extra fullness is generally desirable. Press the seams open or to one side; topstitching is optional.

3. Hem the sides of the curtain first. Press, then fuse or stitch 1" (2.5cm) double hems—see pages 71 – 72.

4. Stitch the casing. If using a 1" (2.5cm)-round rod, press under 1/2" (1.3cm), then press under 3" (7.5cm). The total casing is 3-1/2" (9cm). Stitch 2-3/4" (7cm) from the fold. For other casing calculations, see page 71.

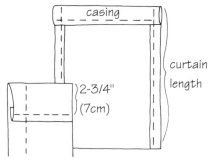

5. Insert the rod through the casing and install. Check the length. Mark the hem and take the curtain down. Press, then fuse or stitch 3" (7.5cm) double hems—see page 71. In a hurry? Just glue or fuse the hem in place, while it's up.

6. *Optional:* Secure to one side with a tieback—see page 17. *Variation:* Crisscross two curtains from a double rod.

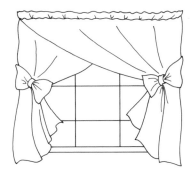

Versatility Plus: Shirred Variations

• Divided curtains. This more traditional style may better suit your taste or wider window size. When calculating yardage—see page 85—use the fuller 2-1/2 to 3:1 ratio. Divide the fabric lengths required as follows: If you need two lengths, place one on each side; three lengths, one and one-half on each side; four lengths, two on each side. Sew and hem each side of the divided curtain as described for single-panel shirred curtains—see page 16.

• Top ruffles, also known as "headings." Allow extra length when calculating curtain yardage (twice the ruffle depth—see page 85). Fold under the casing plus the ruffle width and stitch the ruffle width from the fold. The second row of stitching will form the casing.

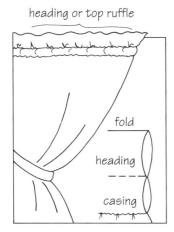

heading or top ruffle

fold

heading

casing

• Tiebacks. For *a tied tieback,* use ribbon, cording, filled bias tubes, or self-fabric ties, at least 36" (90cm) long. Fasten a small cup hook to the wall or window frame. Thread the tieback through a small ring, hang it from the hook, and tie.

For *wider tiebacks that wrap,* use ribbon, decorative trim, or edge-finished fabric strips, 2" – 4" wide by 16" – 22" long (5cm – 10cm wide by 41cm – 56cm long). Try on the curtain before trimming to the finished length. Hand sew or *zigzag* a small ring to the center of each end, and hang both from the hook. *Variations:* Embellish the edges—see pages 74 – 75. Or braid together three cords—see *Fasturn®*, pages 80 and 93.

For soft, lavish tiebacks, use swag holders—see page 28—and at least 3 yards (2.7 meters) of fabric. Narrow the width of the fabric if the tieback is too full.

For the fastest tieback, choose from the many ready-mades.

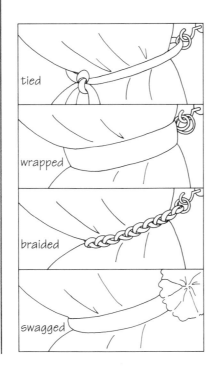

tied

wrapped

braided

swagged

• Sashes. Add extra length for two casings and two ruffles. See "Top ruffles," at left. The sash is either mounted inside the frame, usually with tension rods, or just outside the frame with café or sash rods. *Optional:* Tie the center together with a ribbon, sash, round ring, or *Infinity Ring*.

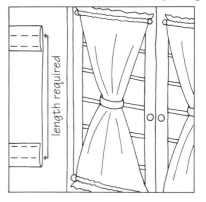

length required

• Lined curtains. Cut and piece the lining the same as the curtain. Before hemming the sides, pin the curtain and lining right sides together and sew as one layer.

For heavier fabrics, the lining should be sewn separately. *Option 1:* Buy a double-rod, make a separate lining curtain, and hang on the inside rod. Or use lining tape—see page 18. *Option 2:* Hem the lining separately, 1-1/2" (4cm) shorter, 1" (2.5cm) narrower. Center lining and curtains wrong sides together. Fuse the lining to the curtain along the side hems; then stitch the casing as one layer.

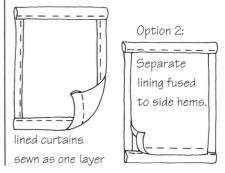

lined curtains sewn as one layer

Option 2: Separate lining fused to side hems.

Easy-Does-It Decorator Tape Tips

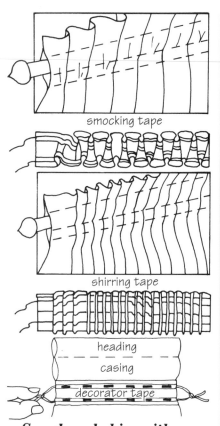

smocking tape

shirring tape

heading

casing

decorator tape

• **Smock and shirr with sew-on decorator tapes**—see page 78. Follow the recommended fullness ratio guideline when cutting out the curtain. Cut the tape the unfinished width plus 3" (7.5cm) for allowances. Press under the casing. If there is a top ruffle, stitch the first row from the fold. *Place the tape below the casing,* folding under 1-1/2" (4cm) on each end. Lap the loop side of the tape over the casing edge. Stitch to secure the upper tape edge and form the casing. Then stitch the lower edge of the tape. *Be careful not to catch the cords in the stitching. Also, to prevent the cords from being pulled out, knot the cords securely at each end.* Pull up the cords from each end, arranging the fullness, and wrapping to secure the cord tails. Insert the rod, adjusting the fullness and tugging the hem to set the drape.

• *Replace sewing with fusing*—see pages 76 and 78. Use iron-on tapes, following the label instructions. *Reminder:* Cut the fusible tapes to length without allowances, finishing the ends with seam sealant. *For a totally no-sew treatment,* fuse seams—see page 72—and hang the curtain with iron-on hook-and-loop tape applied above the decorator tape and fastened to a mounting board—see page 79—or the frame.

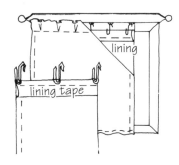

iron-on tapes

decorator

hook & loop

• *Coordinate tiebacks.* For 3-1/2" (8.8cm) finished width, cut a strip 6-1/2" (16.3cm) wide by 2 – 2.5 times the length needed. This will be from 40" – 54" (100cm – 140cm). Press under all edges 1-1/2" (4cm). Center smocking or two-cord shirring tape over the edges and stitch in place. Draw up the cords and sew on rings—see page 17.

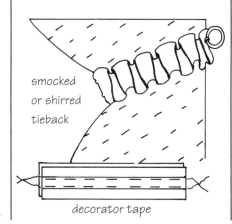

smocked or shirred tieback

decorator tape

• *With lining tape, add a separate lining* for light control, insulation, and uniformity. Close the curtains to measure. *For width,* add 1-1/2" (4cm) ease for every foot of rod, plus 4" (10cm) for side hems. *For length,* measure from the rod to the hem plus 2" (5cm). Cut out and piece. Stitch or fuse 1" (2.5cm) double side hems and a 2" (5cm) double lower hem. Sandwich the top edge of the lining between the tape and the fabric; stitch through all layers. Hang from the existing hooks, or from drapery pins on a separate traverse rod.

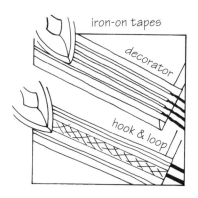

lining

lining tape

• *Pleat perfectly* with sew-on or fusible tapes. *For width,* multiply by the recommended fullness ratio, such as 2.5. Then add 3" (7.5cm) for each return—the rod-end wrap—and the center-front overlap if applicable, plus 2" (5cm) at each side for 1" (2.5cm) double hems. *For length,* add 3" (7.5cm) for the top hem plus 8" (20cm) for a 4" (10cm) double hem.

total fabric width = (2.5 x rod width) + returns, overlaps, & hems

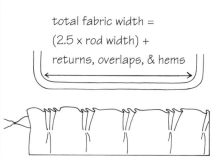

Yes, Casingless Curtains

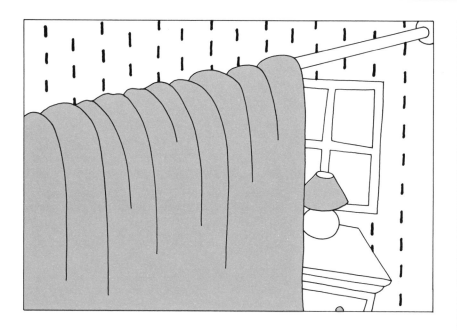

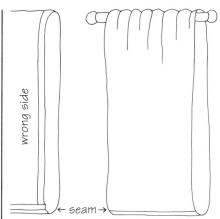

A curtain with no casing? Sounds easy, you say, but perhaps a bit amateurish looking? Fortunately, the casingless methods described here don't compromise results. Lavishly draped and instantly self-lined, they can be room dividers and shower curtains, too. Or scale down the curtain size and hang in a doorway—perfect for puppet shows.

The Materials

• *Fabric:* Just about any weight or type of fabric. *Avoid one-way designs,* if a change in motif/nap direction, front to back, is objectionable. *For the circle curtain,* you'll need 9-1/4 yards of 45" width to cover an area 30" wide by 79" long in a 2:1 ratio (8.4 meters of 115cm width to cover an area 76cm wide by 200cm long in a 2:1 ratio). *To calculate for either the circle or draped style,* see page 85; double the length (A), add 6" (15cm) ease/fit insurance, eliminate casing (C) and hem (B) allowances, and for draped curtains, add 40" (102cm) to (A) for puddling.

• *Hardware:* Any rod adjustable to or cut to the desired width—see page 80. Tension rods are easiest to install and reposition.

• *Optional:* For circle curtains, *weighted tape or chain.* For draped curtains, one large rubber band. For both, tiebacks—see page 17.

The Steps for Circle Curtains

1. Cut the total yardage into the number of lengths necessary. *Optional:* Press or fuse under, or serge-finish the lengthwise edges. Selvages will usually suffice as edge finishes.

2. Fold each length in half, right sides together, and hang over the rod. Allowing for a 1/2" (1.3cm) seam along the raw edges, mark to shorten as necessary. Remove and stitch the seam. Turn right sides out. Repeat for any additional lengths. *Piecing the lengths together is not essential.* The unseamed edges are hidden in the fullness, and can later be divided into any configuration.

3. Insert the rod through the curtain, arranging the fullness evenly. If the seamline is conspicuous, position it at the top edge, rather than along the hem. *Optional:* Run weighted tape or chain through the inside of the hem fold to minimize billowing.

The Steps for Draped Curtains

1. See Step 1 for Circle Curtains.

2. Place the fabric over the rod to create the curtain. To "hem" the ends, reach in from the sides, finger-fold the two layers right sides together, and wrap with a rubber band. Arrange in an elegant puddle on the floor. *Variation:* Mark to the length desired, either to the floor or puddled, and edge-finish or hem—see pages 72 – 73.

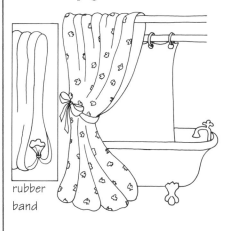

rubber band

More Instant-Curtain Innovations

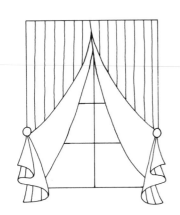

• **Double-tent flaps or "kerchief curtains."** Cover the window with two pillowcase shades—see page 24. Form a casing and hang from a rod, fasten with a mounting board—see page 79—or staple directly to the frame. *Variations:* Instead of lining each panel, use a lace, sheer, or hefty double-sided fabric, and edge-finish with serging, binding, or narrow hemming—see pages 72 – 75.

• **Curtains à la shades.** Draw up simple shirred curtains into cloud-like configurations. Draw up the center with a ribbon or self-fabric tab, 8" – 10" (20.3cm – 25cm) long. Sew from front to back, embellishing with a button or tassel. For movable tabs, add button, snap or *Velcro®*. Similarly adapt a shirred valance—see pages 26 – 27.

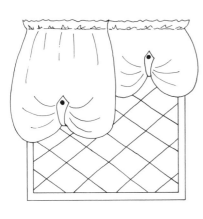

• **Quick cafés.** Providing both light and privacy, this shirred style covers only the lower third or so of the window. A companion valance is optional. *Variations:* Hem the top and hang from clip-on café rings spaced evenly apart. Or sew decorative rings directly to the top hemmed edge and hang from a rod or hooks; arrange a reversible curtain randomly on and off the hooks for a casually elegant look.

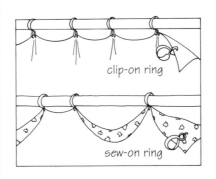

clip-on ring

sew-on ring

• **Crisscrossed curtains.** Drape the measuring tape to estimate the length, adding 20" (51cm) for each knot or rosette. Make two shirred panels, crossing them and knotting. Either push-pin in place or pull through swag holders—see pages 28 and 80.

• **Self-rosette tieback curtain.** Transform the look of lace, lined, or reversible shirred panels. Hand gather the lower inside corner of the panel into a rosette, fastening with a rubber band—see page 76—and tack back. Or form the rosette tieback by pulling through a swag holder—see pages 28 and 80. *Optional:* Add 20" (51cm) to each panel length. Adjust the length from the top *after forming the rosette;* then stitch the casing.

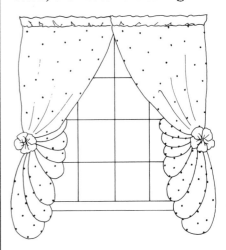

• **Tack-ups.** Mount flat or shirred curtains with evenly spaced decorative tacks. Wide-width fabrics and sheets work wonderfully for this treatment. Hem only the crosswise edges.

Match a Wall-Covering

Insulate Instantly & Inexpensively

3

SIMPLY SENSATIONAL SHADES

Cover Creatively

Fake a Roman Shade, Fast

Super-Simple Roller Shades

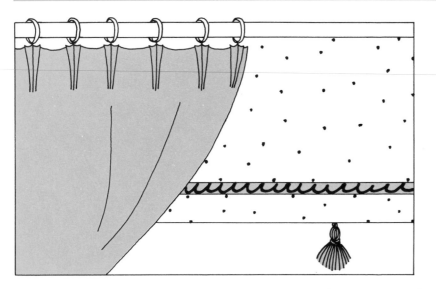

Rather press than sew? Looking for a close-to-the-window treatment that helps control drafts and blocks light? Short on fabric? If you answered "Yes" to any of these questions, consider roller shades. The key ingredient—the backing material—is now readily available, easy to apply, and affordable.

The Materials

• **Fabric:** Any fade-resistant, mid-weight cotton. You will need 1-3/4 yards of 54"-wide fabric for a window 30" wide by 52" long (1.6 meters of 140cm-wide fabric for a window 76cm wide by 132cm long). For other yardages, see page 85. *Caution:* Water-repellant fabrics can resist fusing. Test first.

• **Fusible backing:** *Fuse-A-Shade*™ by HTC or *Shade Maker*™ by Dritz, both 45" (115cm) wide; *Wonder-Shade*™ (light blocking) by Pellon, 42" (106cm) wide; or any similar product. Yardage will be the same as for the fabric.

• **Shade roller and hardware:** For either an inside or outside mount—see page 80. Should include *slat,* either wood or plastic, cut to the width of the finished shade. Reuse the original slat if replacing a shade.

• **Staple gun**

• **Optional:** *Shade-pull ring or cord; seam sealant or white craft glue* to finish the vertical edges; and *trim* to embellish the lower edge.

The Steps

1. Steam press the fabric to remove any residual shrinkage. Then cut the desired width plus 2" (10cm) by the length plus 12" (30cm). Cut the backing material the same dimensions—also, see page 22.

2. Following the manufacturer's instructions, fuse the backing to the fabric. For the smoothest bond, fuse on a large, continuous surface, such as a cutting or ping-pong table. Let the shade cool completely before removing. *Optional:* If using *Fuse-A-Shade*™ or *Shade Maker*™ (not *Wonder-Shade*™), have it fused by a dry cleaner. You can press-baste first, in a few spots.

3. Carefully trim the fused shade, cutting a 1" border in from all edges. *Optional:* Run a fine bead of white glue or seam sealant along the vertical edges, or serge-finish.

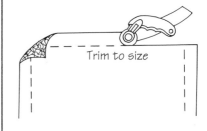

Trim to size

4. Press up a 1-3/4" (4.5cm) hem. Sew or fuse a 1-1/4" (3cm)-wide pocket or whatever is needed to fit the slat.

5. Check the roll direction of the roller. With tape, position the top edge of the shade on the roller; it must be straight to roll straight. After straightening, use a staple gun to securely fasten the shade.

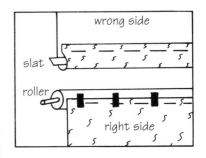

wrong side

slat

roller

right side

6. Install the roller hardware, and hang the roller and the shade.

Optional: Attach a pull ring or cord, or glue or fuse trim above the hem.

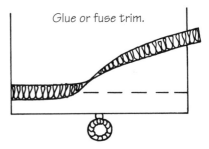

Glue or fuse trim.

Shortcut Shademaking

Roller-Shademaking Tips
(Refer to how-to's on page 22.)

• **Test-fuse** 1/4 yard (.23 meter) of the backing material on the shade fabric. Determine the optimum fusing procedures: time, amount of steam, with or without a pressing cloth. Practice marking and cutting smooth, straight lines, with a sharp utility knife, rotary cutter, or shears.

• **If using Fuse-A-Shade™ or Shade Maker™,** hem the edges. Cut the backing 2" (5cm) narrower than the finished shade width. After fusing the backing to the fabric, use transfer-web strips to fuse the fabric hem allowances to the shade backing.

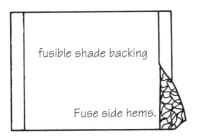

fusible shade backing

Fuse side hems.

• **Piece horizontally, close to the roller,** if the shade is wider than the backing. *Wonder-Shade™* edges can be butted, but nonwoven fusibles should be lapped about 1/8" (3mm).

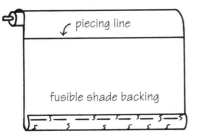

piecing line

fusible shade backing

• **Press from the fabric side if using Wonder-Shade™.** When fusing dress-weight fabrics, press over each area only once to prevent adhesive bleed-through. After the shade has cooled completely, pin-puncture

any bubbles on the backing side, and re-press these and any unfused areas.

Tension-Rod Shades
• **Instantly install tension-rod shades,** without any carpentry whatsoever.

1. Choose the shade style: one-rod (top), two-rod (top and bottom), or three-rod (top, center, and bottom). Rods should fit inside the frame.

2. Cut the fabric the inside-frame dimensions plus casing and hem allowances. For top and bottom casings, allow the rod diameter plus 1-1/2" (4cm) each. Allow 3" (7.5cm) for the two 1-1/2" (5cm) side hems. For a center casing, cut a separate piece of fabric the rod diameter plus 1" (2.5cm) by the inside window width plus 1" (2.5cm), or substitute wide bias hem tape. Stitch or fuse the hems and casings as shown.

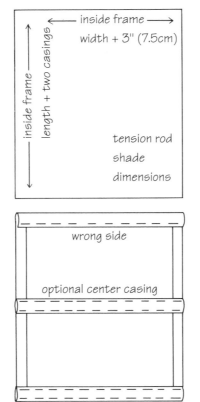

inside frame width + 3" (7.5cm)

inside frame length + two casings

tension rod shade dimensions

wrong side

optional center casing

Optional: Line the shade. Place the fabric and lining wrong sides together and sew as one layer. A layer of insulating interlining—see page 79—can be the lining or can be sandwiched between the fabric and a lining.

3. Install the shade in the position desired. It can easily be moved to an alternate position; just release the rod tension, move, and reactivate the tension.

arrows = rod placement

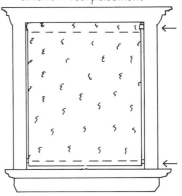

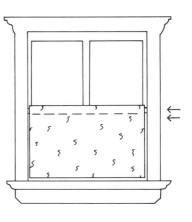

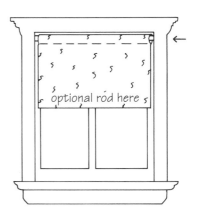

optional rod here

More Shades Made in Minutes

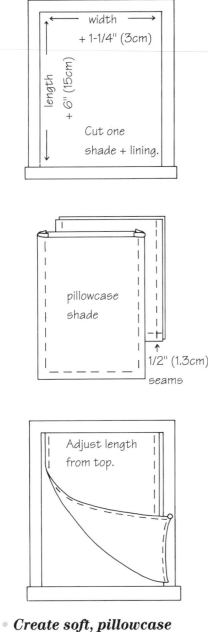

width
+ 1-1/4" (3cm)

length
+ 6" (15cm)

Cut one
shade + lining.

pillowcase
shade

1/2" (1.3cm)
seams

Adjust length
from top.

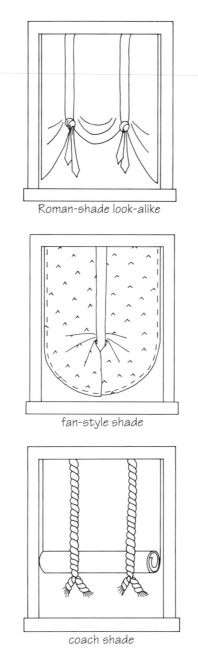

Roman-shade look-alike

fan-style shade

coach shade

strap length. Install as instructed for pillowcase shades. Tie to the desired height, trimming the strap length as necessary. *Optional:* Fuse, glue, or stitch the strap for a few inches at the top of the shade. *Variations:* **Fan the lower edge** by using only one strap in the center. Add an additional 24" (61cm) in length when cutting out the shade. Tie to form the fan, then cut the shade to the desired length and mount. ***Or roll up a coach shade.*** Cut a dowel or PVC pipe the pane width. Insert inside the open end of the pillowcase shade. Roll either up or under and tie to the length desired.

• ***Make it tubular!*** Refer to "Circle Curtains"—see page 19—but cut the shade in a 1:1 ratio. Hang as is, or tie Roman- or fan-style (see center column).

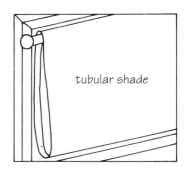

tubular shade

• ***Staple fabric on stretcher bars that fit inside the frame.*** Cover all or just part of the window with sheers, laces, graphics, or even bug screening.

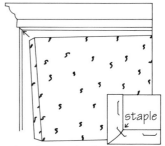

staple

stretcher-frame shade

• ***Create soft, pillowcase shades.*** Cut either two layers of fabric or the fabric and a lining to the unfinished size desired, as shown. Wrong sides together, stitch three sides and turn. Topstitching the finished shade is optional but recommended because it flattens the edges. Form a casing and hang from a rod or mounting board. Or staple directly to the frame, buffering with upholsterer's tape. See pages 79 – 80.

• ***Vary the pillowcase style, easily.*** Allow an additional 12" in length. For Roman-shade look-alikes, cut two pieces of ribbon, webbing, or finished fabric strips, each twice the shade length plus 2 yards (1.8 meters). Place the midpoint of both straps at the top of the shade, spacing them about half the shade width apart. Try tying to different heights on the window before trimming the

**Beautify Blinds
With Easy, Inexpensive Toppers**

Frame With No-Sew Fabric Flourishes

4

VERY EASY VALANCES

**Double Decorating Drama
With Teamed Treatments**

**Accent Without Blocking
Light or the View**

Quick-Shirred Valance & Variations

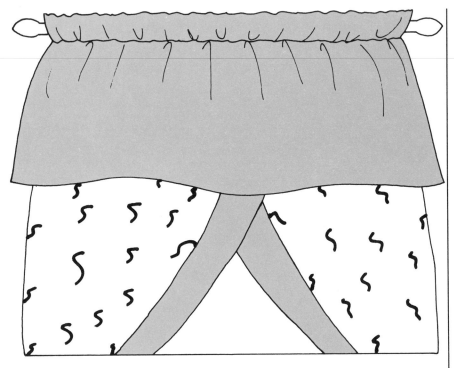

Simply a shorter version of their curtain cousins, shirred valances are equally versatile and easy-to-make.

The Materials

- **Fabric:** Any light- to mid-weight cotton. You will need about 1-3/8 yards of 45"-wide fabric for a finished valance shirred to 40" wide by 15" long in a 2:1 ratio. (You will need 1.3 meters of 115cm-wide fabric for a finished valance shirred to 102cm wide by 38cm long in a 2:1 ratio.) Consider railroading to eliminate piecing—see page 81. *In doubt about valance length?* The standard is about 15" (38cm) finished. Cut yours a few inches longer and hang unhemmed. Try several lengths before marking the hem. For custom calculations, see page 85.
- **Hardware:** Any rod adjustable or cut to the desired width—see page 80. If the valance will be used in tandem with a curtain, a double rod works well.
- **Optional:** *Lining.* The yardage will be the same as for the valance.

The Steps

1. Follow Steps 1 – 6 of "Quick! Shirred Curtains," on page 16. *Variations:* Add a top ruffle—see page 16. Make a short-sash valance by adding both a top and lower-edge ruffle.

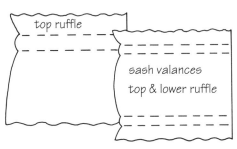

top ruffle

sash valances
top & lower ruffle

- **Quick-copy the cloud look.** Cut the valance 1.5 – 2 times the length desired. Construct as usual. Tie with two ribbons or edge-finished fabric strips, about 3 yards (2.7 meters) long. Space the ties about half the full width apart. *Fast variation:* From either side, hand-pleat and secure with a rubber band.

Tie into cloud look.

Rubber-band rosettes
either right or wrong sides.

- **Or create the cloud look with decorator tapes**—see pages 18 and 78. Cut the valance 2 – 2.5 times the length desired. To draw up the valance, use shade or two-cord shirring tapes spaced half the full width apart and sewn or fused vertically or at an angle.

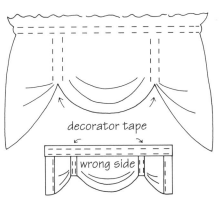

decorator tape

wrong side

Shirred Genius: Valance Versatility

- **Smocked or shirred.** Center decorator tape on a sash-style shirred valance—see page 26. Fuse or sew the tape in place and draw up the cords to fit the finished width. *Variation:* Make the basic shirred valance, but fuse or sew shirring or smocking tape below the casing—see page 18.

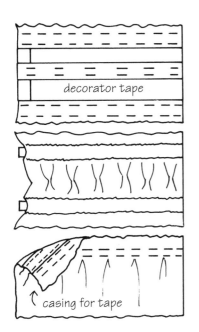

decorator tape

casing for tape

- **Bustled.** Fuse or sew shade or shirring tape—see pages 18 and 78—to draw up the sides. *Very-easy variation:* Draw up into rosettes with *Infinity Rings* or rubber bands.

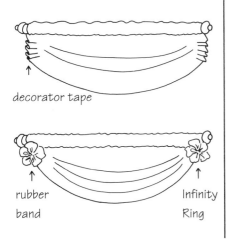

decorator tape

rubber band

Infinity Ring

- **Poufed.** Double the finished length below the rod without the hem; add 2" (5cm) ease and the casing/heading allowances—see page 16. Fold up the excess length, lapping 1/2" (1.3cm) under the casing edge. Stitch casing. *Optional:* Stuff the pouf with tissue.

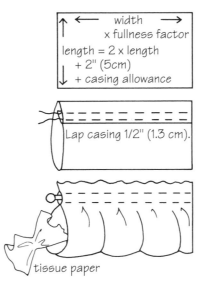

width →
x fullness factor
length = 2 x length
+ 2" (5cm)
+ casing allowance

Lap casing 1/2" (1.3 cm).

tissue paper

- **Double-rod poufed.** Double the length below the rod, add for two casings (top and lower) and one heading (top). Usually the lower casing is shirred on a tension rod, so that it can be easily positioned. Adjusts to fit a range of window heights. *Optional:* Stuff pouf with tissue.

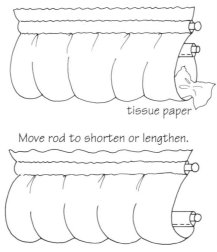

tissue paper

Move rod to shorten or lengthen.

- **Shirred-curtain-to-valance conversions.**

Tie back a shirred curtain up to one corner, instantly creating an asymmetrical cascade valance. *Variation:* Secure and rosette cascade corner with a rubber band or *Infinity Ring*.

Drape extra long shirred panels on a decorative rod, in one of many intriguing designs—see "Window-Scarf Yardage Tips," page 85.

No-slip tip: Use a push pin or stick-on *Velcro®* to prevent slippage of the casing.

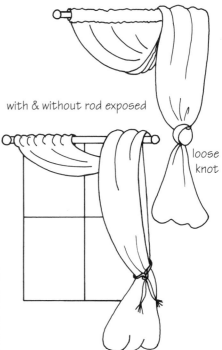

with & without rod exposed

loose knot

No-Sew or Nearly-No-Sew Scarves

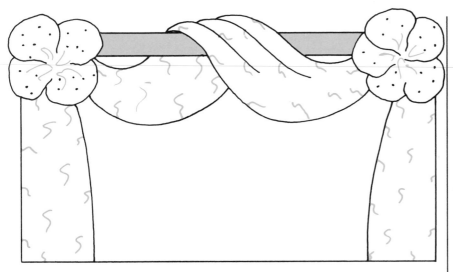

There's no faster way to professionally frame a window. Borrowed from quick-change store displays, the fabric is draped, swagged, and puddled, with little or no sewing. More benefits: Scarves can be removed, recycled, or restyled, instantly.

The Materials

• **Fabric:** Any fade-resistant, mid-weight fabric at least 45" (115cm) wide or wider. Wider widths will drape more lavishly. For fuller scarves, double the width by seaming two 36" or 45" (90cm or 115cm) fabrics together along the selvage. Also remember to double the yardage requirement. For a scarf puddled at both hems to frame a 36" by 60" (90cm by 150cm) area, you will need 6-1/2 yards (5.9 meters) of any width fabric. For other yardages, see pages 84 – 85.

• **Swag holders and/or rods,** such as those by Claesson, Graber, Kirsch, or Repcon—see page 80. Or substitute holdbacks, small wreaths, towel hangers, and round or oval picture frames.

• **Optional:** *A drapery/curtain rod or mounting board,* used in place of or in addition to the swag holders.

The Steps

1. Position the swag holders and/or rod first. Ask a friend to help measure. Use a carpenter's tape measure or cording to measure, simulating the drape. Remove and measure the tape or cording. Calculate yardage as shown on page 85, adding for all rosettes, knots, sleeves, and puddled hems. If in doubt, *cut longer* because it's difficult to salvage a too-short scarf.

2. Cut the scarf length. If piecing is necessary, try to position the piecing seams to be hidden in a rosette, wrap, sleeve, or tieback.

← Hide piecing seam.

3. If the fabric has a contrasting color selvage, press under and fuse or stitch. *Optional if using a 54" (140cm) or wider fabric:* Fold in half lengthwise, seam, and turn the tube right side out.

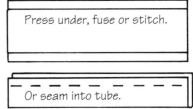

Optional:

Press under, fuse or stitch.

Or seam into tube.

4. Find the center of the scarf, and push-pin it to the center of the frame. Then start draping. If the scarf is drooping, push-pin or staple to the frame, rod, or mounting board. Adding another holder or rod in the middle is an option suggested for 40" (102cm) and wider expanses.

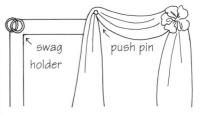

swag holder — push pin

5. Hem without taking down the scarf: Glue in position or move your pressing equipment or machine close enough to fuse or stitch. *For puddled hems,* hand-pleat and rubber-band. When hemming tubes, open the seam about 30" (76cm) above the hem; reach inside to hem.

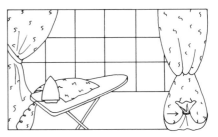

Hand-pleat and rubber-band.

Scarf-Design Sketchbook

Note: To estimate additional yardage for knots, poufs, rosettes, and sleeves, see page 85.

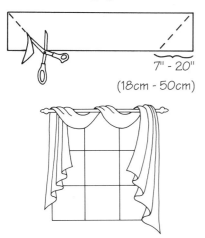

7" - 20"
(18cm - 50cm)

• **Taper the scarf ends** for a graceful, off-the-floor cascade. The taper generally angles from shorter on the inside to longer on the outside, as shown. When working with scarves sewn in a tube, center an opening in the seam, stitch the taper, trim, and turn through the opening.

• **Fully line the scarf,** by sewing two lengths right sides together along the selvages. Taper the ends—see illustration above.

• **Combine two or more fabrics in one scarf,** a wonderful no-sew way to achieve a more lavish drape with lighter-weight or narrow-width fabric. Some holders have extensions specially designed for holding a second or third scarf.

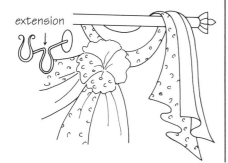

extension

• **Pull through a pouf or two.** *Optional:* Stuff with tissue. Some holders should be pulled apart to place the loop, and then pinched together to secure the loop base.

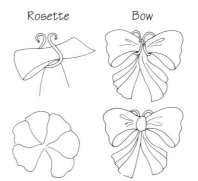

Cover hardware with pouf.

• **Fan a rosette.** Pull one or two loops through, fan the fabric, and hide the ends to form a circle. *Optional:* Pinch a small pouf to hide any hardware. *Bow variation:* Don't fan the loops all the way out.

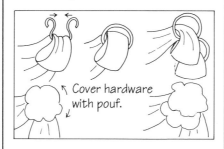

Rosette   Bow

• **Drape a Bishop sleeve** a few inches below the holder. *Optional:* Stuff with tissue paper. *Variation:* With *Infinity Rings,* pull through two loops for double flounces.

No-slip tip: Double-wrap around the holder extension or ring.

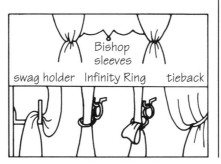

Bishop sleeves

swag holder   Infinity Ring   tieback

• **Embellish with a no-sew rosette.** Fold in the corners of a 15" – 25" (38cm – 68cm) square or napkin or hand-pleat the edges of a similarly sized circle. Poke in the center of a swag rosette for accent. *Optional:* Rubber-band to secure.

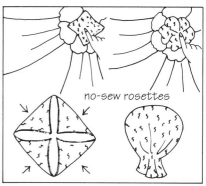

no-sew rosettes

• **Echo the scarf drapes,** or tie back with elegant satin cording finished with tassels.

• **Loosely knot the scarf** at the corners or over swag holders. For a fatter knot, insert a layer of fleece or batting before knotting.

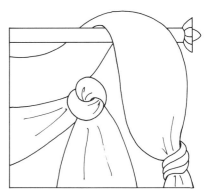

More Timesaving Window Toppers

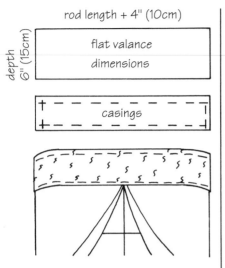

rod length + 4" (10cm)

depth 6" (15cm)

flat valance dimensions

casings

• **Fashion a flat valance.** Position two rods the finished valance depth apart. Cut a piece of fabric the rod length, including the curved "returns," plus 4" (10cm)—for 2" (5cm) each double side hems—by the valance depth plus 6" (15cm), or two casing allowances. Fuse or sew the side hems and casings and insert the rods. *Optional:* For more body, fuse shade backing to the fabric—see page 80.

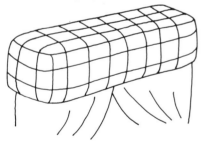

• **Cover cornice kits with fabric,** kits such as *Window Crowns by Beverly*—see Designer Touches, Inc., page 93. Sewing and carpentry expertise are not prerequisites for making these professional-looking, light-weight upholstered valances.

• **Take advantage of valance fabric by the yard.** All are edge-finished or hemmed on at least one long side; some even have casings on the other.

• **Substitute garlands for valances.** Use a fabric-filled garland, such as *Garland-Decor* from Repcon—lap and bend to the shape and size desired. Or use any garland suited in style and size to the window and decor. Embellish with bows, ribbons, and dried flowers.

Garland Decor

• **Let table linens do double duty.** Use staples or *Velcro®* to attach a runner to the mounting board—see page 79—or directly to the frame; the extra length drapes gracefully at the sides. Fold fringed napkins or pretty pillowcases diagonally over the valance rod. Or drape a round lace tablecloth over the rod, tying at the corners.

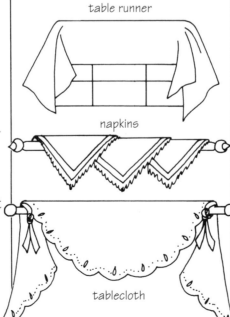

table runner

napkins

tablecloth

• **Shirr sleeves.** Cut the fabric the rod circumference plus 2" (5cm), which includes ease and seaming, by 2 – 3 times the rod length. Don't piece—make enough sleeves to shirr together, hiding the rod. Stitch a 1/2" (1.3cm) seam, right sides together, turn, and shirr on the rod, tucking under the end edges.

Optional: Position two or more wide, sleeved rods together. Add double the ruffle width for each heading. *Pro tip:* Add a short 1" (2.5cm) ruffle to the top of the lower rod, to cover any spacing between. *Variation:* Make one large sleeve, with stitching down the center, to house two rods.

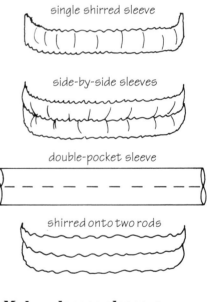

single shirred sleeve

side-by-side sleeves

double-pocket sleeve

shirred onto two rods

Make a looser sleeve, a valance version of the "Circle Curtain" on page 19. *Variation:* Use two rods, the second used to weight, fill, and stabilize the lower-edge fold.

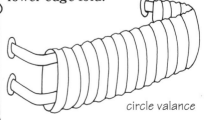

circle valance

Finally, Custom-Fit Covers, Fast

Discover Sheetcase Conveniences

5

BEST-BET BED COVERS

*Copy Designer Looks
(Without Spending Designer Prices)*

Dress the Bed & the Bedroom

Quick, Comfy Comforter

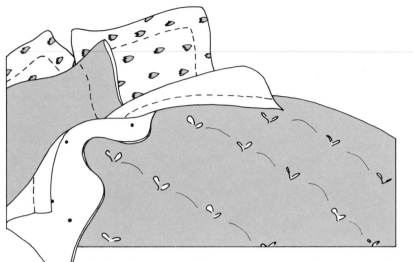

This lofty batting-filled cover can be easily completed in one short sewing session. My dear friend and well-known PBS-TV hostess, Nancy Zieman, developed the innovative turning technique, which secures the batting (without basting!) while turning the comforter right side out.

The Materials

- **Fabric:** Any mid-weight, basic-color. Wide-width fabric or sheets are suggested. *For each side of a double size,* you'll need one king sheet or 9 yards of 45"-wide fabric, 3 yards of 90"-wide fabric (8.2 meters of 115cm-wide fabric, 2.7 meters of 230cm-wide fabric). For other yardages and calculations, see pages 86 – 87.
- **Batting:** Two or three layers, with outer dimensions of 84" by 94" (213cm by 240cm). Suggested loft is 3" (7.5cm) or a total weight in layers of 8 to 12 ounces. For example, two layers of 6-ounce (170 gram) batting equals 12 ounces (340 grams). For more about batting, see page 78.
- **Yarn:** For tying tufts, one small skein or ball of crochet or pearl cotton, or lightweight worsted yarn.
- **Long, large-eyed handsewing needle:** For tufting.

The Steps

1. Cut the necessary number of lengths from the total yardage required *for both sides.*

2. Piece to avoid a seam running down the center of the comforter—see page 71. Trim to the desired unfinished dimensions, allowing 1/2" allowances on all sides. Try the pieced cloth on your bed to double-check the size. Remember, some of the length and width will be taken up by the batting loft—see page 87. *Optional:* Round the corners—see page 71.

Note: Work on a large, flat, clean surface, such as your living room floor, when cutting, marking and tufting.

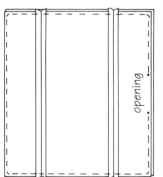

3. With tailor's chalk or an erasable marker, mark the top layer for tufting, spacing the marks no more than 10" (25cm) apart.

4. Lay top and bottom fabric right sides together, with piecing seams aligned if applicable. Stitch around the outside edges with a 1/2" (10mm) allowance, leaving a 36" (90cm) opening, as shown.

5. Trim the batting to the *finished* shape and dimensions of the comforter. Place the batting on one side of the comforter.

6. To turn the comforter right sides out, roll the corners opposite the opening toward the batting side, then through the opening. Ask a friend to help.

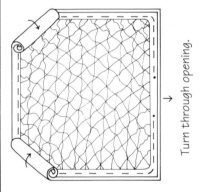

Turn through opening.

7. Blindstitch the opening closed by hand. To secure the layers, tuft with 8" (20cm) lengths of yarn, tying as shown. Trim the yarn tails as desired. *Optional:* Tuft by machine, bartacking at the markings.

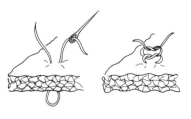

One-Session Sheetcase

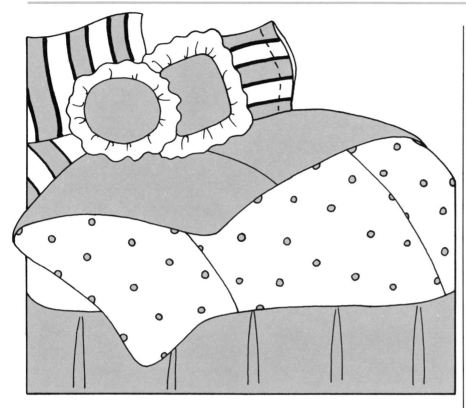

A sheetcase or duvet cover is like a giant pillowcase for your comforter.
Fast to make, it offers two other distinct advantages: One, it hides any
color or condition of comforter inside, and two, once on the bed, the
comforter requires only seconds to neaten.

The Materials
• **Fabric:** Any durable, tightly constructed mid-weight fabric or
sheets. For yardages, refer to the "Quick, Comfy Comforter," page 32.
For other yardages and calculations, see pages 86 – 87.
• **Lining:** Any durable, tightly constructed fabric that is care- and
weight-compatible with the top fabric. Yardage will be the same as for
the fabric.
• **Zipper:** Used here, one long standard-weight zipper about half the
finished width of the sheetcase. Consider buying the zipper by the
yard—see page 80. Or buy two zippers, centering the pulls in the
middle of the opening.

The Steps
1. Use a comforter you already own or make your own—see Step 1
for the "Quick, Comfy Comforter" on page 32.

2. If necessary, piece the comforter top and lining—see page 71.

3. Center the comforter on the wrong side of the fabric. Trace the
edge of the comforter on the fabric. Trim along the markings. *Do not
add seam allowances*—for the lush, overstuffed look, the finished
cover should be slightly smaller than the comforter. Mark and trim
the lining in the same fashion.

4. Center the zipper along one of
the short ends and mark the top
and bottom position. Right sides
together, stitch a 3/4" (2cm)
seam to the markings, basting
across the zipper opening. Insert
the zipper.

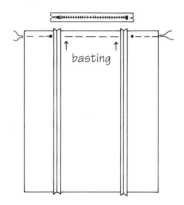

5. Open the seam and zipper.
Right sides together, stitch a 3/4"
(2cm) seam along the remaining
three sides. Trim the corners
and turn right sides out.

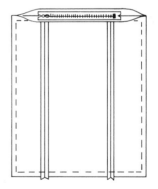

6. Put the comforter inside its
cover. If it slips around too much,
turn the sheetcase wrong sides
out and use fat rubber bands to
secure the corners.

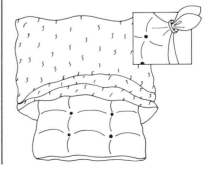

Throws: Tailored & Timeless

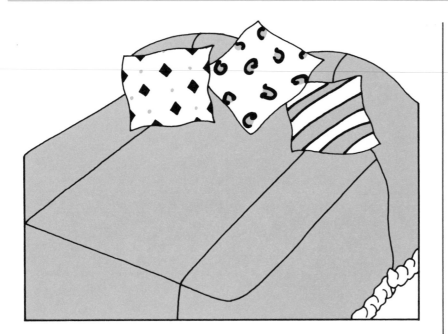

Throws aren't just for hotel beds. Full-length and long enough to cover the pillows, they eliminate the need for shams or a skirt. The all-in-one look is quite elegant, perfect for a contemporary bedroom.

The Materials
• **Fabric:** Any mid- to heavy-weight. Wider widths are suggested. *For a double size,* you'll need 10-1/4 yards (9.4 meters) of 45"(115cm)-wide fabric or 6-1/2 yards (5.9 meters) of 72" (180cm)-wide fabric. For other yardages and custom calculations, see pages 86 – 87.

The Steps
1. Cut the necessary number of lengths from the total yardage required.

2. Piece to avoid a seam running down the center of the throw—see page 71. Trim to the unfinished dimensions, allowing 2" (5cm) allowances on all sides. Try the pieced cloth on your bed to double-check the size. *Optional:* Round off the two corners at the foot of the bed—see page 71.

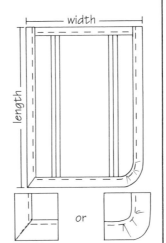

3. Finish the hem edges, trimming or turning up 1/4" (5mm). Press 1-3/4" (4.5cm) hems to the wrong side, easing if there are rounded edges, or mitering corners. Topstitch 1-1/2" (4cm) from the hem or fuse.

Variations
• **Lined throw:** Speed hemming, while adding weight and body.

1. Follow Step 1, allowing only 1/2" (1.3cm) for seaming the outer edges. Cut out and piece both a top and lining; leave a 10" (25cm) opening centered in one of the lining seams. To make the lining slightly smaller than the top, trim 1/4" (5mm) from the outer edges.

2. Place the top and lining right sides together, aligning the piecing lines, pinning intermittently to secure the layers. Lay on a clean floor large enough to accommodate the project flat. Double-check to make sure the lining is about 1/4" (5mm) smaller on all edges than the top; if not, trim as necessary. Round two corners, as shown below.

3. Stitch around the edges, allowing a 1/2" (2.5cm) seam. Turn right sides out through the lining-seam opening. Close the opening with hand blindstitching. Align the piecing seams of the top and bottom, securing by stitching in the ditch, from the top side. Topstitch the seamline along the outer edge of the throw.

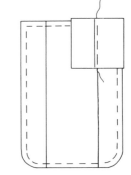

• **Welted or ruched throw:** Align the welting or ruching stitching line with the unlined throw hemline, restitch, turn, and topstitch. Or for the "Lined Throw," insert the welting in the top/lining seam—see page 75.

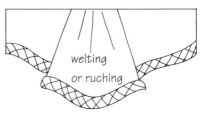

welting or ruching

Remarkable Reversible Quilt

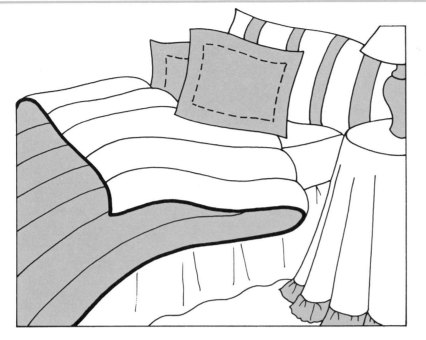

Even for quilting novices like me, reversible-strip quilting is a cinch and the results, wonderfully practical. The top, batting, and lining are sewn or serged together simultaneously, creating an insulated cover that's durable and launderable.

The Materials

- **Fabric:** Any firmly woven mid-weight. Refer to the throw yardages and calculations on pages 82 – 83. To add for the extra seams, simply use the yardage estimate for the next size larger bed—i.e., for a queen bed, use the king-size yardage. When custom calculating the total width needed, allow for the extra seams by adding 1/2" (1.3cm) for every 9" (23cm) in unfinished width required.
- **Batting or fleece:** Any weight and type desired—see page 78. Yardage will be the same as for the top fabric.
- **Lining:** Any firmly constructed light- to mid-weight care-compatible fabric. Yardage requirements will be the same as for the top fabric.

The Steps

1. Cut the fabric, batting, and lining into the lengths required—see estimates/calculations for throws on pages 88 – 87. Cut all the lengths lengthwise, into strips.

For maximum yield, cut 36"-wide fabric into four 9" strips; 45" width into five 9" strips; 54" width into six 9" strips; 60" width into seven 8-1/2" strips; 72" width into eight 9" strips; 90" width into ten 9" strips; and 120" width into fourteen 8-1/2" strips.
(Cut 90cm-wide fabric into four 23cm strips; 115cm width into five 23cm strips; 140cm width into six 23cm strips; 150cm width into seven 21.5cm strips; 180cm width into eight 28cm strips; 230cm width into ten 230cm strips; and 300cm width into fourteen 21.5cm strips.)

2. Make the first "squilt" (Robbie Fanning's word for a quilt sandwich): Place the batting between the wrong sides of a top and lining strip. Pin and then baste through all layers 1/4" (6mm) from the edges.

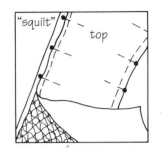

3. On both sides of the squilt, place a top and lining—top right sides together and lining right sides together. Pin. Then place a batting strip on the wrong side of the top strip. Align the edges and straight stitch or serge. Create the second squilt row by folding the top and lining right sides out, sandwiching the batting between. Machine-baste the edges together and repeat this step until the pieced quilt measures *at least* the unfinished width required.

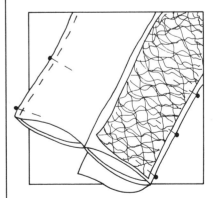

4. See the hemming how-to's on page 34. *Variation:* Welt or ruch the edge—see page 34—or trim the hems and bind the edge—see page 74.

Speedy Shams and Cases

Comforters and most quilts aren't designed to cover the pillows. With shams, it's easy to complete the bed "dressing." Update the look of your bed and bedroom quickly and affordably simply by changing the shams and skirt—see page 37.

The Materials

• **Fabric:** Any mid- to heavy-weight with a high-thread count. *For the ruffled sham, 2-1/2 yards (2.3 meters) of 45" (115cm)-wide fabric. For the plain sham, 1-1/8 yards (1 meter) of 45" (115cm)-wide fabric. For the flanged sham, 1-1/2 yards (1.4 meters) of 45" (115cm)-wide fabric. All yardages are for standard-size pillows. Also see pages 77 and 87.*

The Steps

1. Cut out the sham pieces. Place the length parallel to the crosswise grain, except when cutting a king-size sham out of 36" (90cm)-wide fabric.

2. Double-hem the center-back openings of the two back pieces, turning 1" (2.5cm) each time. Fuse or topstitch the hems about 3/4" (2cm) from the folded edges.

3. Overlap the two back pieces 2" (5cm) or to match the size of the front sham, right side up. Pin the overlaps. Pin the front and backs right sides together, and stitch a 1/2" (1.3cm) seam. Wrap corners or trim to minimize bulk. Turn right side out.

Variations

• **Ruffled sham:** Piece strips into a length two to

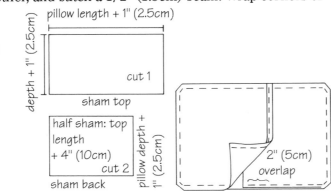

three times the perimeter of the sham. Gather; pin to the front, distributing the gathers evenly.

• **Flanged sham:** Suggested for firm, mid- to heavy-weight

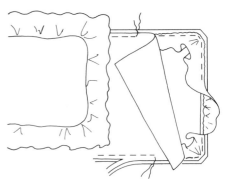

fabrics. Add 6" (20cm) to the depth and length of the front and both back pieces. After Step 3, topstitch 3" (7.5cm) from the seamed edge to form the flange.

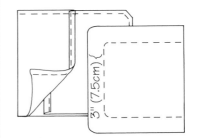

• **Pillowcase:** Cut out the case—for dimensions, see page 77. Double-hem one end as shown, turning 4" (10cm) each turn, and topstitch or fuse. Fold the case in half, lengthwise, and sew or serge the seam.

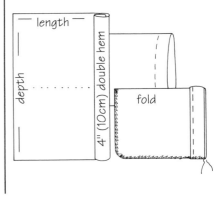

Instant On-&-Off Bed Skirt

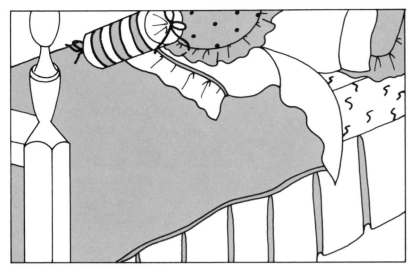

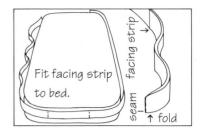

Fit facing strip to bed.

facing strip

seam

↑ fold

5. With a 1/2" (1.3cm) seam, sew the raw edge of the strip to the skirt, right sides together, and topstitch. Safety-pin the facing strip to the box-spring sheet.

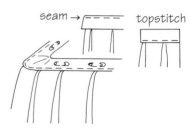

seam → topstitch

Bed skirts, also known as dust ruffles, beautify box springs while hiding all sorts of storage under the bed. They can be effortlessly removed for a decor change or laundering.

The Materials
- **Fabric:** Any light to mid-weight fabric. You'll need 5-1/2 yards (5 meters) of 45" (115cm) width for a three-sided double-size skirt. For other yardages, see page 86.
- **Folding or two-cord shirring tape:** From 12 – 15 yards (11 – 13.7 meters) when using sew- or iron-on tapes with 2 to 2.5:1 fullness ratio—see page 78.
- **Facing strip:** 1 yard (.9 meter) of inexpensive, tightly woven mid-weight. *Variation:* 7 yards (6.4 meters) of 2" (5cm) bias facing.
- **Large safety pins:** About 25 – 30.

The Steps
1. Cut the number of crosswise strips required—see page 86. Piece strips together along the short ends.

2. Fold up a 2" (5cm) double hem along one of the long skirt edges. To hem, topstitch from the right side, blindstitch from the wrong side, or fuse. Fold in 1" (2.5cm) hems on both ends of the strip; topstitch or fuse.

3. Place the tape along the wrong side of the unhemmed edge; *make sure the drawstring is on the outside.* Edgestitch or fuse. Tie the cords at one end and pull them from the other end.

4. Cut the facing fabric into 6" (15cm)-wide crosswise strips. Piece the short ends together. Try the strip on the bed, cutting to the correct length plus 1/2" (1.3cm). Fold the strip in half, right sides together, and sew the two short ends wrong sides together with a 1/4" (6mm) seam. Turn right sides out.

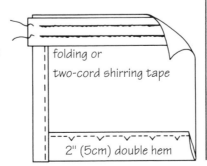

folding or two-cord shirring tape

2" (5cm) double hem

Variations
- **Tension-rod skirt:** Instead of seaming the short ends of the facing strip, fold them under. Insert a tension rod, and suspend it between a headboard and footboard or posts.

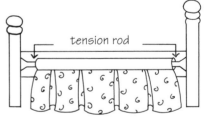

tension rod

- **Serge-finished or bias strips.** Cut 3" (7.5cm)-wide facing strips, and serge-finish all sides. Or substitute 2" (5cm) purchased bias facing. Overlap the skirt 1/2" (1.3cm) and edgestitch.

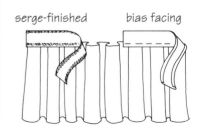

serge-finished   bias facing

More Best-Bets for Beds

● **Swagged headboards.** Drape a fabric over tiebacks, rosettes, or swag holders secured to the wall—see page 80. Puddle the ends, hemming with rubber bands—see page 76.

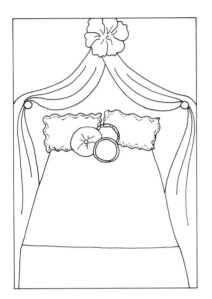

Or hang a rod or a plant hanger or shelf bracket on the ceiling or wall, centered above the head of the bed. Fold your fabric in half lengthwise, wrong sides together. Drape over the hardware, selvages against the wall. Secure to the wall. Knotted tiebacks are shown here—see page 29. Puddle ends or hem.

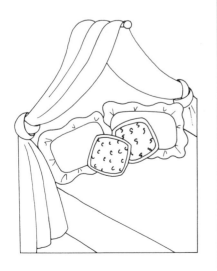

● **Fabriced headboard.** Use one of the methods shown in Chapter 8, pages 52 – 56, using *Quik Trak*™, stapling, or shirring.

● **Wall-hung headboards.** As a base, use easy-to-cut, lightweight foamboard—see page 79. Cut the base to size, pad with batting, wrap with fabric, and staple—see page 56. Fasten to the wall with brads (headless nails), picture-hanging hardware, or carpet tape.

Instant solution: Buy a headboard kit, like the one sold by London Fabrics—see "Sources," page 94.

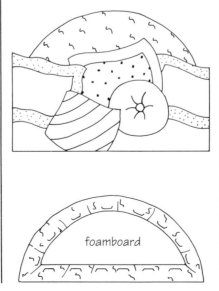

foamboard

● **Skirt it, without sewing!** Fold your fabric in half, lengthwise, wrong sides together, and press. You'll need about 6 yards (5.5 meters) for a three-sided double-bed size skirt. Safety-pin to a sheet on the box spring: Wrap around the box spring, adjusting to fit the length and perimeter. To finish the ends, tuck them in or wrap them out of sight.

For no-sew swags, thread the fabric through 1" – 2" (2.5cm – 5cm) rings; safety-pin the rings to the skirt and box-spring sheet.

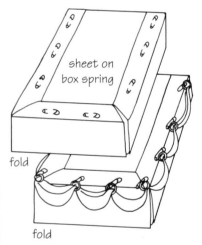

sheet on box spring

fold

fold

● **Sew sheets out of wide-width fabrics.** Contour the corners for fitted sheets or hem edges for flat sheets. See sizes and cutting guidelines on page 77.

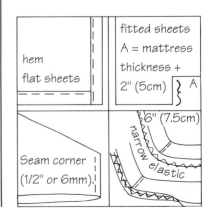

hem flat sheets

fitted sheets
A = mattress thickness + 2" (5cm) } A

Seam corner (1/2" or 6mm).

6" (7.5cm)

narrow elastic

Salvage Outdated or Worn Furniture

Let Runners Protect, Accent, & Camouflage

6

EASIEST SLIPCOVERS EVER

**"Upholster" Chairs Yourself,
Affordably & Fast**

**Soften Tailored Lines,
Transform Utility Furniture**

Drawstring-to-Fit Cushion Covers

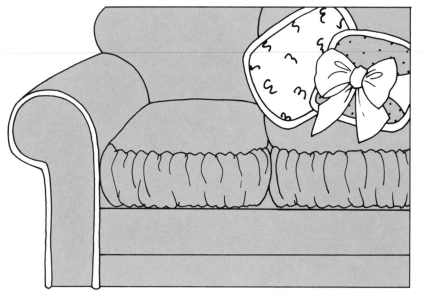

This cover is always snug, without time-consuming pin-fitting. Combine this cushion-cover style with fast-to-make throws—see page 41. The neat, tight fit lends an almost-upholstered look to the draped couch.

The Materials

• **Fabric:** Mid-weight, tightly constructed. For a 22"-square by 4"-deep cushion, you will need 1-3/4 yards of 45"-wide fabric. (For a 56cm-square by 10cm-deep cushion, you will need 1.6 meters of 115cm-wide fabric.) For custom calculations and other yardages, see pages 88 – 89.

• **Cushion:** Firm round, square, or rectangular shape, at least 3" (7.5cm) deep. *Caution:* Too-soft cushions can compress.

• **Drawstring cord:** 3 yards (2.7 meters) per cushion of 1/4" (6mm)- round elastic bungie cord, which is a smaller diameter version of bike tie-down cords, sold in upholstery- or outdoor-supply stores. If unavailable, substitute 1/4" (6mm) cording or clothesline, or 3/4" – 1" (2cm – 2.5cm) garment elastic.

• **Optional:** 22" (56cm) square per cushion of *sew-in or fusible fleece*, as a buffer layer—see page 78.

The Steps

1. Cut the total yardage into the tops and side strips required—see pages 88 – 89.

2. Seam to piece the strips together. As a casing opening, leave one of the piecing seams open for the last 1-1/2" (4cm). Press the seams open. Turn under 1-1/2" (4cm) and stitch 1-1/4" (3cm) from the fold to form the casing.

3. Gather the long edge of the strip opposite the casing. *Optional:* Fuse fleece and/or machine quilt the cushion top.

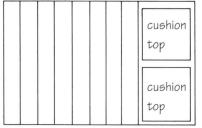

layout example: side strips & tops

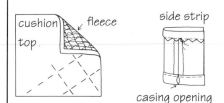

4. To distribute the gathers evenly, divide the perimeter of the top edge of the cushion by the number of side strips, and mark with pins. Pin the side strip to the cushion top, matching pins to seams, wrong sides together. Stitch the 1/2" (1.3cm) seam.

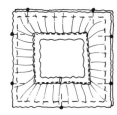

5. Thread the elastic or cording end through a bodkin or large bobby pin, then work through the casing. *Optional:* Cover the underside of the cushion with fabric. Hand baste with long stitches to the original cover.

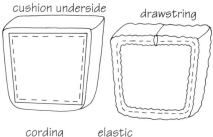

6. Place the cover on the cushion, right side out. Draw up the shirring until the fit is snug. Tie the elastic in a knot to secure. If using cording, tie in bow for easier untying. *Don't trim off the tie tails!* They are needed for removal of the cover, so tuck them under the shirring.

Throws: Trendy & Terrific

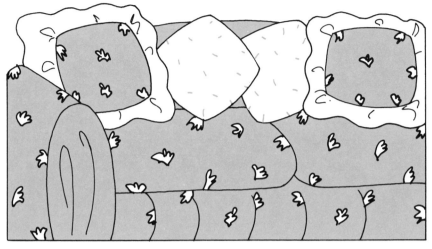

With soft, draped lines and minimal fitting, throws are the quickest-to-make covers. Removable cushions are essential to this easy slipcovering technique: covered separately, the cushions neatly secure the throw.

The Materials
- **Fabric:** Any tightly constructed mid-weight. Consider sheets or wide-width fabrics, so no more than two lengths or one piecing seam will be necessary. For the throw and three drawstring cushions—see page 40—you will need about 12 yards of 60"-wide fabric to cover a mid-sized sofa 80" wide by 30" high (10.8 meters of 150cm-wide fabric to cover a mid-sized sofa 203cm wide by 76cm high). For custom calculations and other yardages, see pages 88 – 89.
- **Upholstery or "twist" pins** (the pointed ends are curlicued): A large box.
- **Optional:** Drawstring-cover materials—see page 40.

The Steps
1. If working with sheets or wide-width fabric, cut to the total width and length dimensions—see page 89. *If working with widths that require piecing,* cut into two lengths; right sides together, selvage to selvage, stitch a 3/8" (1cm)-wide seam to piece the lengths together.

2. Remove the cushions and try the pieced yardage on the sofa or chair. *When working with 45" – 72" (115cm – 180cm) widths,* the piecing seam will probably run behind the seat cushions. *When working with extra-wide fabric,* the piecing seam may run along the top edge. *When working with more than one print sheet,* the piecing seam will be camouflaged even if centered vertically.

3. Fit the throw into all crevices. Use upholstery pins in areas that will be hidden under the cushion or drapes. Replace the cushions. "Hem" by tucking the excess fabric under the furniture; leave as is, or secure with upholstery pins or T-pins, or staples. *Optional:* Mark a 1" (2.5cm) hem. *Without removing the cover,* fuse by sliding a sleeve board along the edge, or glue it.

Variations
- **Buffer the furniture** with fleece—see page 78. Before covering, secure with a few upholstery pins.

- **"Gift wrap" cushions**—see page 44.

- **Control corner fullness.** Tie in place with ribbon or webbing. Or thread ties through grommets. Or fold hospital-style and pin, hand baste, or tie in place.

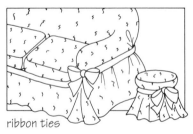
ribbon ties

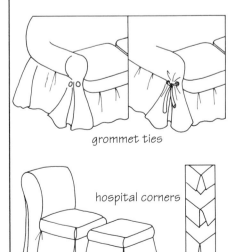
grommet ties

hospital corners

Furniture Runners to the Rescue!

Seldom does the entire chair or sofa demand to be slipcovered. With very little fabric, sewing expertise, or time, runners add much-needed camouflage, color, texture, and style.

The Materials

• **Fabric:** Any tightly constructed mid-weight with lots of body, such as double-sided prequilted fabric. You will need about 1-3/8 yards of 45"-wide fabric for a 24" wide by 72" long single-layer runner (1.3 meters of 115cm-wide fabric for a 61cm wide by 180cm long single-layer runner). If making the tubed quilt variation, add extra length for the loft "take-up allowance"; for custom calculations and other yardages, see page 85.

• **Optional:** If machine quilting the fabric, use *lining and bonded batting, fleece, or 1/4" (6mm) thin foam*—see page 70. Yardages will be the same as for the same-width fabric—see page 88. If binding the edges, you will need 5-3/8 yards (4.9 meters) of *wide quilt binding* or 2" (5cm)-wide *bias self-fabric strips*. If serge-finishing, consider *decorative thread* for the upper and/or lower loopers—see page 73.

The Steps

1. Cut out the fabric to the width and length desired. Economize by cutting out on the crosswise grain and piecing in an inconspicuous area. *Optional:* Line or machine quilt the fabric—see page 70.

2. Try the runner on the furniture. Placing runners under cushions prevents slippage. Trim the length and width after positioning the piecing line, allowing either 1" for hemming or no allowance for serge-finishing or binding. *Optional:* Round off the corners—see page 71.

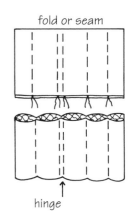
Trim to size.

3. After fitting, remove the runner and either hem by stitching or fusing up 1" (2.5cm) or bind or serge-finish the ends—see pages 72 – 73.

Variations

• **Miter the short ends,** adding tassels for weight and accent—see page 13. *Optional:* Trim the edges with satin cording or piping—see pages 74 – 75.

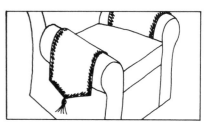

• **"Tube quilt" runners** to soften lawn furniture or hard-surfaced chairs. Follow Step 1 on this page, cutting out a fabric and a lining. Place the fabric and the lining right sides together and stitch a 3/8" (1cm) seam, leaving one long side open. Channel quilt the two layers together, 4" – 5" (10cm – 12.7cm) apart. Stuff the tubes with fiber fill. Keep stuffing and fitting to the chair, until the shape, size, and firmness desired are achieved. Handstitch, machine stitch (with a zipper foot), or bind the opening closed.

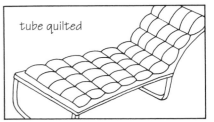
tube quilted

fold or seam

hinge

"Upholster" Chairs, Fast

When a chair is only partially upholstered, it's very simple to spruce up with new fabric.

The Materials
- **Fabric:** Any tightly constructed mid-weight. *For four chair seats* 18" wide by 16" long by 3" deep, you'll need 3 yards of 45"-wide fabric. *For four chair backs* 18" wide by 20" high by 2" deep, you'll need 4 yards of 45"-wide fabric. (*For four chair seats* 46cm wide by 40cm long by 7.5cm deep, you'll need 2.7 meters of 115cm-wide fabric. *For four chair backs* 46cm wide by 51cm high by 5cm deep, you'll need 3.6 meters of 115cm-wide fabric.) For other yardages, see page 88.
- **Chairs:** Basic, curved chairs with continuous lines and removable seats.
- **Staple gun and staples:** For fastening the fabric to the underside of the chair seat.
- **Optional:** *Fiber fill and fleece* for filling in seats that have sunk. Each pair of chair seats requires about one 16-ounce (454 grams) bag of fiber fill and 3/4 yard (.7 meter) of fleece.

The Steps for Covering Chair Seats
1. Remove the seat from the chair frame, unscrewing it if necessary. *Optional:* If the seats are sunken, fill in with fiber fill. Smooth the top with a layer of fleece.

2. Cut the fabric for the cover. Using the chair seat as a pattern, add at least the seat cushion depth plus 2" (5cm) on all sides.

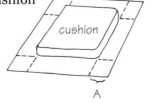

A = depth + 2" (5cm)

3. Working from side to opposite side, staple the fabric to the chair seat. For smooth corners, fold and staple as shown. Finish the raw edges with cloth tape.

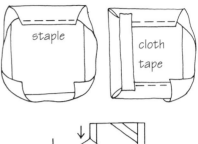

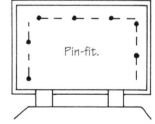

The Steps for Covering Chair Backs
1. Pin-fit the fabric, right side out, on the chair back; the length can be partial or full. Covers for curved backs will have definite back and front sides. Mark the wrong side.

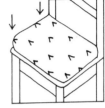

2. Transfer the pin markings to the wrong sides. Trim the seam allowances to 1/2" (1.3cm) and hems to 1" (2.5cm). Use this pattern for any additional covers.

3. Stitch the seam and topstitch or fuse the hem. Turn right sides out. Slip cover over chair back.

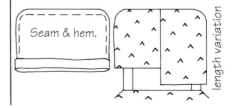

More Instant Slipcovers

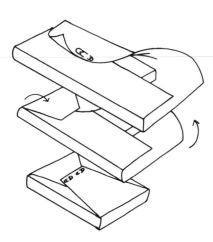

- **"Gift wrap" cushions.** Wrap cushions with fabric as you would presents with gift paper. For fastening, use large safety pins. Most cushions require 1-1/2 to 2 yards of 45" – 60" fabric (1.3 meters of 115cm to 150cm fabric) or a rectangle that measures twice the width plus 6" (15cm) and twice the length plus 6" (15cm).

- **Slipcover a stool, chair, or ottoman** with a round table-cloth—see page 9—controlling fullness with a bow, tie, or an *Infinity Ring*. To estimate the best size, measure over the stool, chair, or ottoman, adding *at least* 30" (76cm) for tying and puddling. Try on the stool and tie before marking the hem.

- **Slipcover section-by-section.** Cover the arms first, then the center section in one or two pieces. For some less-than-60" (150cm)-wide fabrics and for more precise alignment of hems, this method offers advantages.

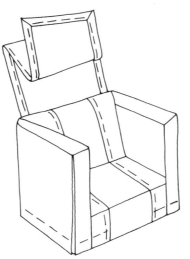

- **Skirt throw and ottoman slipcovers.** First safety-pin or baste the throw to the upholstery. Gather with an elastic casing, decorator tape, or *Stitch 'n Stretch* elastic sewn or fused to the skirt-top hem. If necessary, fasten the skirt with hook-and-loop tape.

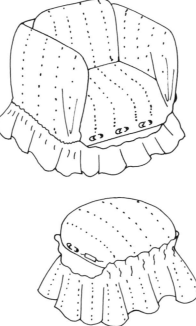

- **Skirt covers for wood or metal chairs, too.** Pad the chair with one or two layers of bonded batting or fleece, first loosely hand basting the batting to the chair. Drape a large rectangle over the chair, controlling the fullness at the legs with elastic, rubber bands, or hand basting. Gather, lap, and fasten the skirt as described above for skirt ottomans.

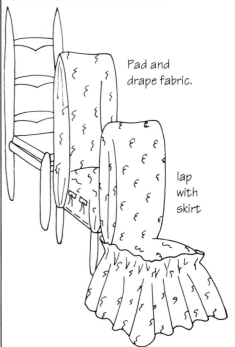

Pad and drape fabric.

lap with skirt

- **Drape a runner**—see page 42—over a chair back. Secure with a tasseled cord, ribbon, or fabric sash.

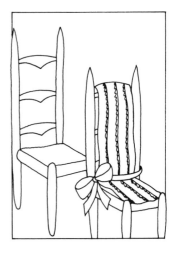

Coordinate Colors & Fabrics in Room

Lend a Cozy Look to a Bed or Couch

7

PILLOW & CUSHION
POSSIBILITIES

Create Floor Furniture

Transform Everyday Pillows
for Holiday Decorating

Knife-Edged Pillows, Plus...

A Better Basic Pillow

Round corners.

} 1/4" (6mm)

1. Using the desired dimensions—see page 77—cut out the pillow top. To prevent too-pointy corners, quarter-fold the top and round the corners; use as a pattern for the back piece.

2. Place the top and back right sides together. Stitch together with a 1/2" (1.3cm) seam allowance, wrapping the corners—see page 72—and leaving an opening centered in one side that measures about half the side of the form. Turn right side out through the opening.

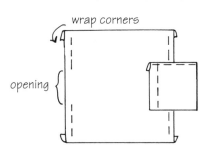

wrap corners

opening {

3. Insert the pillow form into the cover. Handstitch the opening closed or edgestitch, continuing around the pillow edge.

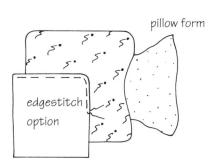

pillow form

edgestitch option

Variations

• **For softened, "Turkish" corners,** wrap with rubber bands, as shown, before stuffing or inserting the form.

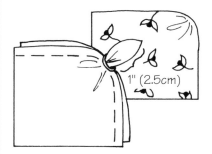

1" (2.5cm)

• **For bandless boxed corners,** measure and mark as shown. Bring the marks together, and baste by machine or hand or with basting tape inside the seamline. Proceed with Step 2.

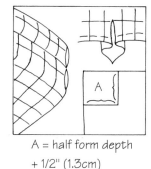

A

A = half form depth + 1/2" (1.3cm)

• **Plan for a zippered or sham closure**—see page 77—if cover removability is a priority. Insert the zipper or lap the sham before sewing the two sides together. Proceed with Step 2.

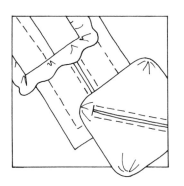

• **Single-flange the edge, super-fast.** Add 5" (13cm) to the length and width of both pillow sides. After Step 2, at left, topstitch 2" (5cm) from the edge, leaving an opening parallel to the side opening. Insert the form, connect the stitching, and close the side as described in Step 3.

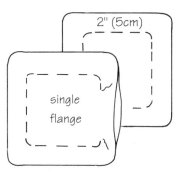

2" (5cm)

single flange

• **Double-flange the edge, fast.** Add 4" (10cm) to the length and width of both pillow sides. Miter all corners—see page 73—and fuse, glue, or tape-baste in place. Place wrong sides together and topstitch 2" (5cm) from the edges. Leave a 6" – 10" (15cm – 25cm) opening centered on one side. Insert the form and connect the stitching. *Variation:* Serge-finish the flanges.

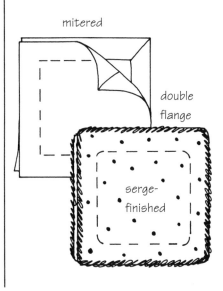

mitered

double flange

serge-finished

Knife-Edged: Easy Embellishments

• **Lavishly ruffled or pleated.**
Soften the look of any pillow,
while enlarging the overall size.
For the fastest ruffles, see page
74. Piece the ruffle into a circle
and quarter-mark. Match
quarter-marks to pillow corners,
but place more gathers at the
corners; pin. Seam the top to the
back. *For the fastest pleats,* piece
into one long strip, then use a
pleater board or pleater
attachment—see pages 70, 79,
and 80. Pin-fit to the edge,
lapping to join.

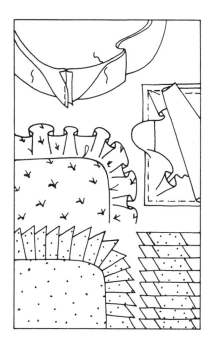

• **"Stuffed" ruffle.** Insert a
continuous batting strip inside
the ruffle before gathering. Cut
the batting strip the ruffle length
by the finished ruffle width. Do
not join in the seam.

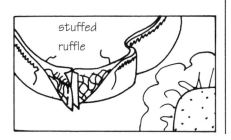

stuffed
ruffle

• **Perfectly piped or welted.**
Baste piping or welting to the
pillow front; apply as shown on
page 75. Compact-ease at the
corners, as shown. Clip the
corners and notch curves, as
shown. Place the pillow pieces
right sides together, and stitch
directly over the basting line.

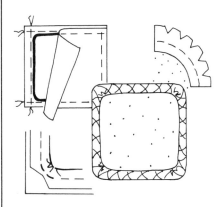

Easier-embellishment tip: For all
these pillows, I allowed for a
zippered- or sham-back closure—
see page 77. That way, no side
opening is necessary, and the
edge embellishment is applied
more uniformly by machine.

• **Really ruched.** Apply
ruching to the pillow top as
described for "Perfectly piped or
welted," above. For ruching how-
to's, see page 75.

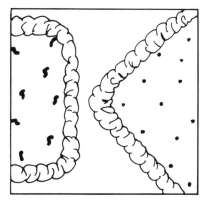

• **Faux-welted.** Add twice the
cording diameter to the length
and width of both sides. Round
the corners—see page 71. Seam
right sides together; turn right
side out. Pin the cording inside
the pillow, pushing it snugly
against the seam. With a zipper
foot and from the right side,
stitch close to the cording,
leaving a 3" (7.6cm) opening.
Pull the cord ends until the edge
is slightly ruched. Cut, butt, and
tape the cord ends. Topstitch to
connect the stitching lines.

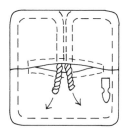

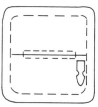

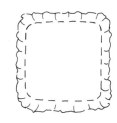

• **Knotted embellishment** by
cohorts Naomi Baker and
Tammy Young. Make a 45"
(115cm) by 13" (32.5cm) pillow
and stuff lightly. Then simply
knot loosely.

Not for Squares Only

• **Copy best-selling bow pillows.** Make a rectangular knife-edged pillow—see page 46—about 18" by 20" (46cm by 51cm). For the center "knot," cut one 8" by 17" (20cm by 43cm) strip of fabric; press fusible fleece to the wrong side but not in the seamlines. Fold the strip in half lengthwise, right sides together, stitch, center the seam, and stitch one short end. Turn right side out, wrap around the center of the pillow parallel with the shorter side and handstitch in place. The more overlap, the fuller the bow. *Variation:* Wrap two pillows into a double bow.

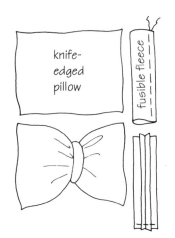

knife-edged pillow

fusible fleece

• **Make rounds.** Cover round pillow forms, following the knife-edged how-to's—page 46. No form? *Plumper-round-pillow tip:* Pull any inserted trim tautly, when applying.

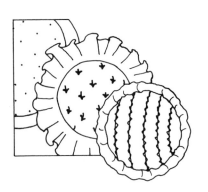

• **Wrap up a no-sew bolster.** Cut a rectangle the bolster length plus 12" (30.5cm) by the fabric width—but no wider than 45"–54"(115cm – 140cm) maximum. Roll the fabric over the form, turning under the exposed edge. Rubber-band the ends, creating rosettes by tucking the raw edges in. *Optional:* Cover the rubber bands with ties. *Sewn variation:* Cut the fabric 6" (15cm) shorter in length and line it, accenting with piping, welting, or decorative serging. Rubber-band the ends.

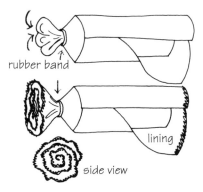

rubber band

lining

side view

• **Fast, basic bolster.** Cut the fabric as shown above. Fold in half, right sides together, and stitch a 1/2" (1.3cm) seam, leaving 1" (2.5cm) openings at

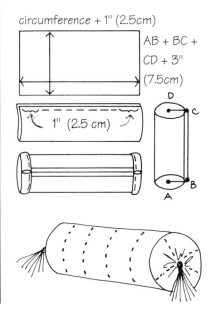

circumference + 1" (2.5cm)

AB + BC + CD + 3" (7.5cm)

1" (2.5 cm)

D
C
B
A

each end. Turn under a 1-1/4" (3cm) casing on each end, and stitch 1" from the fold. Thread a 36" (91cm) length of elastic, cording, or decorative ribbon through each casing. Turn the cover right side out. Center the bolster inside and draw up the ends. The tails can be tucked in or exposed.

• **Smock or shirr a bolster.** Multiply the circumference by 2.5, and cut out as shown for the "Fast, basic bolster" at left. Center the tape and stitch or fuse *before seaming.* Proceed from "Fold in half," under "Fast, basic bolster." Pull up the tape before turning the bolster right side out.

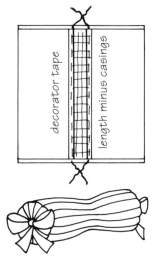

decorator tape

length minus casings

• **Instant ideas:** *No bolster form in sight?* Simply roll up fleece or batting any length or diameter desired. Glue or hand baste the last lap. Or use a twin-size batting roll; insert with the bag on, then remove the plastic.

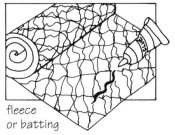

fleece or batting

Savvy Pillow-Seaming Strategies

- **One-piece pillow.** Seam napped or striped fabric into intriguing "patchwork."

1. Cut out a square: 20" (51cm) is required for a 14" (36cm) finished pillow and 27" (69cm) for a 20" (51cm) finished pillow.

2. Fold the square in half, right sides together, and stitch the ends with a 1/2" (1.3cm) seam allowance.

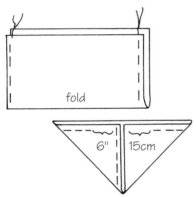

3. Refold, aligning the seamlines. Stitch from each end to within 6" (15cm) of the seamline.

4. Turn right sides out; insert the form. Handstitch the opening closed.

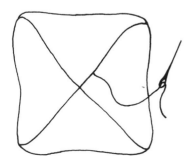

- **Peek-a-boo pillow cover.** An adaptation of the "One piece pillow" at left, this tied-on cover instantly updates any pillow.

1. Cut out a square: A 22" (56cm) size is required for a 16" (41cm) finished pillow. The cover is about one-third larger than the pillow diameter.

2. Cut the binding or ribbon into four 45" (115cm) lengths. Apply to the edge—see page 74—as shown. *Variation:* Instead of binding, serge-finish the edges over narrow ribbon.

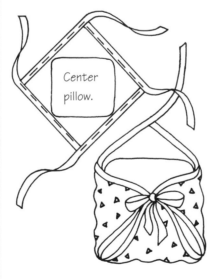

3. Center the pillow on the cover. Bring together opposite corners and tie in bows or the tie style of your choice.

- **Patchwork seaming schemes.** Simple seaming can create design focus from striped, strip-patched, or border-print fabric. For both the chevroned and pinwheel styles, four same-size triangles are required. Remember, seam two triangles together, then the halves. For the pillow back, repeat the design, but allow for the extra when estimating yardage. Or cut a same-size square from leftover or coordinating fabric. Then follow the knife-edge how-to's on page 46.

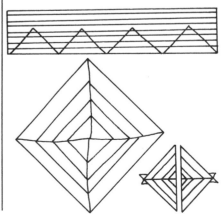

Wow! Pillows in an Instant

• *No-sew wrap-up.* Center a square form on the wrong side of a fabric square 36" – 54" (90cm – 140cm). Bring one corner over the form, fold in the opposite corner, and safety-pin. Bring in the remaining corners and tie. Tuck in or expose tails. Wrap and tuck, or fasten with an *Infinity Ring*—see page 80. *Variation:* Seam the corner ends, as shown, and tie both corners.

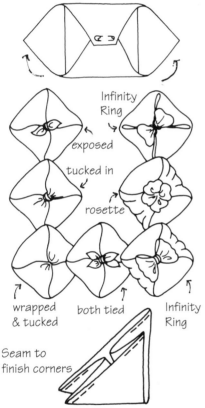

Infinity
Ring

exposed

tucked in

rosette

wrapped
& tucked

both tied

Infinity
Ring

Seam to
finish corners

• *Instant accents.* Wrap with ribbon, lace, trim, scarves, or edge-finished fabric strips.

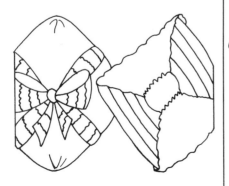

• *Make "pony tail" pillows.* Rubber-band the corners of edge-finished squares, such as napkins, placed wrong sides together over a pillow. Adjust to fit by pulling the tails. Hide the rubber bands with ribbon or decorative cord. Or place the squares right sides together, rubber-band the corners, turn right side out, and insert the form. Reach in to adjust the tails to fit. A tight fit will hide the form; a looser fit will allow a pillow to peek out.

rubber
band

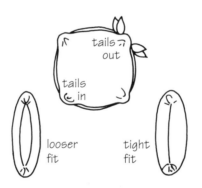

tails
out

tails
in

looser
fit

tight
fit

• *Tie pillowcase pillows* —see page 36. Hide extra pillows, forms, or even fabric(!), beautifully.

pillowcases

• *Rosette a round.* Cut fabric and lining circles 2.5 times the form diameter. Line, accenting the edge with piping, welting, or decorative serging—see page 75. Wrap over the form and rubber-band, arranging the fullness. Disguise the rubber band, if desired, with ribbon or satin cord.

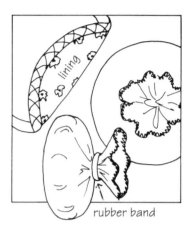

lining

rubber band

• *Quick! Staple a cushion.* Start with a base of hardboard, plywood, or particle board, cut 1/2" (1.3cm) smaller on all sides than the foam form. Use dense foam, 3" to 6" (7.6cm to 15.2cm)-thick; soften with a layer of fleece. Stack as shown. Working from side to opposite side, staple the fabric to the base. Lap the raw edges with cloth tape or cover with a piece of fabric. Turn under the edges, lap, and staple in place.

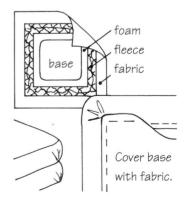

foam
fleece
base
fabric

Cover base
with fabric.

Quickly Cover Outdated Wall Coverings

Replace Messy Paint
With Fuss-Free Fabric

flour

sugar

8

FAST FABRICING

Disguise Decorating Difficulties,
Without Remodeling

Transform Accessories
With Recyclable Fabric

Fabricing Find: Quik Trak®

Besides offering quick installation, this no-sew system requires only common household tools and can cover nearly anything: crummy walls, outdated paneling, or utilitarian corkboard. And of all the methods discussed in this chapter, Quik Trak® fabric applications are the most readily recyclable.

The Materials

- *Quik Trak*®: A box of six 4' (2.2 meters) lengths will frame a 4' by 8' (2.2 meters by 4.3 meters) area; add lengths to cover any area.
- *Fabric:* Any tightly constructed light- to mid-weight. You will need 3 yards of 54"-wide fabric or one twin flat sheet to cover a 51" wide by 96" (8') tall wall area (140cm-wide fabric or one twin flat sheet to cover a 129.5cm wide by 245cm tall wall area). To custom calculate, add 9" (23cm) to the length, by the fabric width. For other yardages and calculations, see pages 90 – 91.
- *Staple gun/staples: For plaster,* use 3/8" (1cm)-leg staples; *for dry wall,* 9/16" (1.4cm)-leg staples. *For large projects,* rent or buy an electric gun, with a flush head for close stapling to the ceiling or corners.
- *Utility or pruning shears:* To easily cut through the track.
- *Level or plumb bob:* For marking true vertical lines.
- *Optional: Batting,* from 2 – 6 ounce (57 – 170 grams) in one or more layers, for the look of lush upholstery plus the benefits of insulation. Yardage will be the same as for the covering fabric.

The Steps

1. With a fine pencil, mark the walls. The vertical markings should measure 3" (7.5cm) narrower than the fabric. If covering the full height of the wall, horizontal markings will be unnecessary—the track will butt against the ceiling and baseboard.

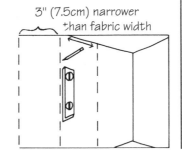

3" (7.5cm) narrower than fabric width

2. Measure, mark, and cut the track to fit the wall. At corners, cut *from the hinge out to the jaw,* at a 45-degree angle. Peel off the backing, position the jaw edge on the marked lines, and press firmly.

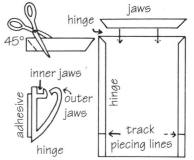

3. Then staple to the surface every 1" – 2" (2.5cm – 5cm), close to the inner jaw. Continue to apply the track for any additional panels. *Optional:* Staple batting inside framed area. Trim any excess.

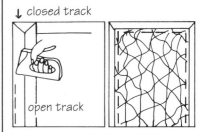

4. Center the fabric over the framed area. *Starting at an upper corner,* insert 1" (2.5cm) into the top channel. Press the channel closed as you tuck the fabric in. Insert the sides, then the lower edge, trimming any excess fabric. Neaten the corners as necessary by reopening the jaws and reinserting the fabric.

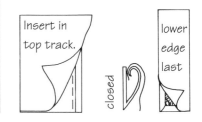

Quik Trak® Quick Projects & Tips

Flash! Just prior to printing, *Craft Trak™* was introduced by *Quik Trak®*. Flatter, without a spacing flange, and sold in shorter 2' lengths (.6 meters), it's designed for smaller projects, mirror and picture frames, album covers, and bulletin boards—see below.

• *Apply track to the back side* of display or bulletin boards, chair seats, headboards, room dividers, or table tops. Recess about 1" (2.5cm) from the edge.

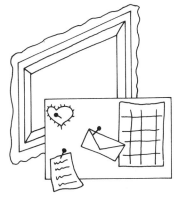

Variation: Mount wall quilts or hangings using the facing-strip application technique, below.

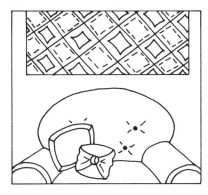

• *Gather fabric for shirred walls,* curtains, or room dividers. Sew on a single-layer facing strip before inserting in the track.

facing strip

• *Substitute Quik Trak® for curtain and valance rods.* Install the track hinge side toward the window, and insert the fabric.

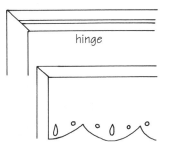

hinge

• *"Railroad" framed areas,* applying the fabric horizontally. Great for display boards, or for protective wainscoting in kids' rooms or kitchens.

Quik Trak

• *Create "reveals,"* leaving spaces between framed areas.

• *Round corners* by simply clipping the *Quik Trak®* every 1" (2.5cm) or so. *Don't clip the inner jaw.* Spread to the curve desired.

Fine-Tuning Walls
• *Don't get cornered.* Complete one inside corner panel; then apply the adjoining frame, jaws open, spacing with a track "tool," as shown below.

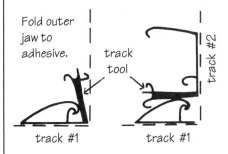

Fold outer jaw to adhesive.

track tool

track #1

track #1

track #2

• *Trim away fabric to expose electrical and switch plates.* Turn off the power; then feel for the outlet, cut away the fabric, and replace the plate.

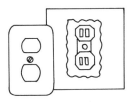

• *"Track" or "block" around doors and windows.*

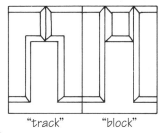

"track"   "block"

• *Hide gaps.* With a screwdriver, slide a 1/4" (6mm)-wide strip of fabric into the channel of the butted track; at corners, use a roll of 2" (5cm)-wide fabric.

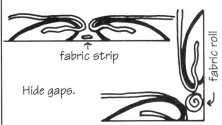

fabric strip

Hide gaps.

fabric roll

Stapling: No-Sew & Cost-Conscious

If your priority is to minimize costs, equipment, and time, consider stapling. Because the fabric is stapled directly to the wall, stapling is most successful over smooth surfaces. For textured or uneven walls, use Quik Trak® or shirring methods—see pages 52 – 53 and 55.

The Materials
- *Fabric:* Any tightly constructed mid-weight. For a 4' by 8' (1.2 meters by 2.4 meters) wall, you will need 3 yards (2.7 meters) of 54" (140cm)-wide fabric or one queen-size flat sheet. For custom calculations and other yardages, see pages 90 – 91.
- *Staple gun and staples:* The light-duty types and 3/8" (1cm)-leg staples work well.
- *Brads:* 1" (2.5cm)-long headless nails. One box would be plenty.
- *Optional:* A *plumb bob or level,* for marking true vertical lines. *Upholsterer's tape,* cardboard strips for straighter seams, available at fabric and upholstery-supply store. Buy 16' (4.8 meters) for each 8' (2.4 meters)-tall panel. *Quarter- and half-round molding,* found in hardware stores, for anchoring corners and covering panel sides. *Clear plastic corner protectors,* bought where wallpaper is sold, for preventing wear on outside corners. *Satin-cord edge* for accenting edges—see page 92.

The Steps
1. Cut the yardage into the necessary number of panels required—see pages 90 – 91. *Matching motifs?* Cut carefully.

2. Determine the placement of the first panel. If working with a large-motif print, center the first panel on the most important wall. Establish a plumb line. Push-pin the fabric panel along the ceiling edge, leaving a 1-1/2" (4mm) hem allowance. Working top to bottom and left to right, staple the panel to the wall every 5" (13cm) or so, pulling it taut as you go.

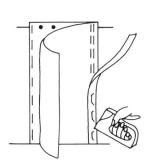

3. Place the second fabric panel over the first, right sides together. Staple along the seam every 5" (13cm). Then cover the stapled seam with upholsterer's tape and staple again, alternating between the first staples. Cut the tape about 1/2" (1.3cm) from the ceiling edge and baseboard. Smooth the second panel across the wall, pulling it taut and repeating the stapling process. The backtacked seam is hidden.

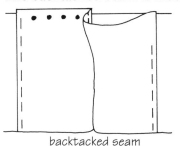

backtacked seam

4. Repeat the backtacking process around the room. To anchor corners, use quarter-round molding that's been painted, stained, or stapled with fabric; nail in place with headless brads.

5. On the last panel, fold under the right vertical seam and tack with small brads. *Optional:* Cover with coordinating half-round molding. At the ceiling and the baseboard, fold under the excess fabric and staple or nail in place with brads. *Optional:* Cover with coordinating quarter-round molding. After securing with push pins, turn off the power; then trim out for wall outlets and switch plates, using a sharp single-edge razor.

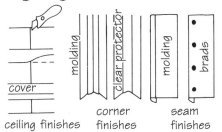

cover	molding / clear protector	molding / brads
ceiling finishes	corner finishes	seam finishes

Shirred Walls: Not for Pros Only

| 1-1/4" (3cm) |
| 1-1/4" (3cm) |
| 1/2" (1.3cm) |

Shirring requires at least twice as much fabric as the other fabricing methods, but it also offers some distinct advantages. The lavish gathers soften any room, while they hide a multitude of decorating dilemmas: pipes, unused windows and doors, ugly paint, retro-textured surfaces and outdated wallpaper.

The Materials

• **Fabric:** Any tightly constructed light- to mid-weight. You will need 8-1/2 yards of 45"-wide fabric or one king-size sheet to cover a 4' by 8' area in a ratio of 2:1 (7.8 meters of 115cm-wide fabric or one king-size sheet to cover a 1.2 meters by 2.4 meters area in a ratio of 2:1). Fabric panels are the desired length plus 7" (18cm) total for headers, casings, hems, and take-up allowance. For other yardages and custom calculations, see pages 90 – 91.

• **Rods or dowels:** 1/2" (1.3cm)-diameter café-curtain rods, wood dowels, or brass rods. You will need sufficient lengths to extend across the wall. If the rod or dowel can bear the weight, it can be cut in one continuous length. If not, butt lengths end to end.

• **Cup hooks:** In a size large enough to hold the rod or dowel— usually 1/2" (1.3cm) size. Purchase six for the first shirred panel and four for each additional panel.

The Steps

1. Cut the yardage into the necessary number of panels required— see pages 90 – 91. *Optional:* If the selvages are white or contrast with the fabric, consider pressing and/or fusing them under first.

2. Press the upper and lower hems 3" (9cm) to the wrong side. To form the heading and casing, stitch 1-1/4" (3cm) and 2-1/2" (6cm) from the fold. This casing is for a 1/2" (1.3cm)-diameter rod. If a different-sized rod is used, double the diameter to determine the distance between the casing stitching lines.

3. Insert rods through the casings. Hold the rod up to the wall and mark for the hook placements between panels; screw the hooks into the wall, "C"-side up, about 1" from the ceiling. If the rod is bowing, support in the middle with additional hooks or small nails. Screw hooks in, "C"-side down, to hold the lower-edge rods.

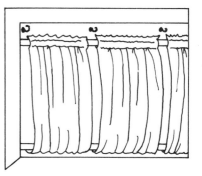

4. Adjust to distribute the shirring evenly, lapping to hide the selvages and openings.

Variation

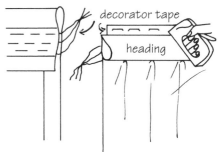

decorator tape

heading

• **Stitch on a wide shirring or smocking tape**—see pages 18 and 78—instead of stitching the casing. Allow the specified fullness ratio when calculating yardage. To fasten, fold back the heading and staple the tape to the wall.

More Fast-Fabricing Ideas

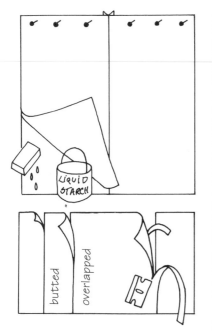

- **Starch fabric to any surface that will tolerate moisture.** (Kudos to Judy Lindahl, fabricing pioneer.) Surprisingly, the fabric can be peeled off, washed, and reused. For best results, use tightly woven cottons; dark colors may show starch residue, which prints generally disguise. Position the fabric temporarily with push pins or tape. Using *concentrated* liquid starch, sponge on the surface, then smooth over the fabric.

To seam, overlap about 1" (2.5cm). Or, butt the edges. Allow 30 minutes or more for drying. Leave overlap as is, or with sharp, single-edge razor blades—the kind sold in paint or hardware stores—and a metal ruler, cut through the center of the overlap.

Test tip: Always pretest starch on your fabric and an inconspicuous wall area.

- *Experiment with adhesives.* With fusible web, fuse fabric to paper, cardboard, or wood. Paint on white glue to permanently adhere fabric to just about any surface, including plastic. Spray-on glues work well, too, but are messy and stinky. Even wallpaper paste, although semi-permanent, works well on most wall-like surfaces.

- *Make movable walls.* Staple fabric over stretcher bars, foamboard, particle board or plywood. *Optional:* Soften with a batting layer. Placed back to back, the fabric-covered bars or boards can serve as room or office-module dividers; hang or prop up between furniture.

Stand-alone fabric-hinged screens are easy, too: Slip foamboard or hardboard between the wrong sides of a cover "hinged" with a double row of stitching twice the depth of the board.

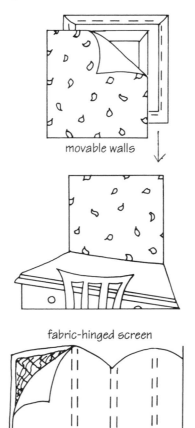

movable walls

fabric-hinged screen

- *Line drawers with paperized fabric*—see page 65. *Optional:* Pink the edges and/or scent with spray fragrance. *Or stick adhesive-backed shelf-liner to fabric*—a new DuPont product, *Fabtac*™, is actually an adhesive-backed *fabric*. Put colored or fabric liner on the wrong side, or clear liner over the right side, to make durable liners.

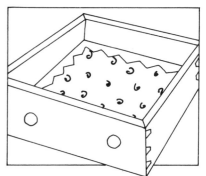

- *Camouflage cheap furniture, shelving, or storage boxes. Staple fabric on utility boxes* to create upholstered tables and seating. Staple fabric to shelving, or to utility tables—see page 11. *"Gift wrap" boxes with paperized fabric*—see page 65—securing with double-sided carpet tape.

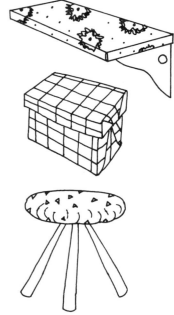

Accent Your Home, Crafts, & Gifts

Make One-of-a-Kind
Ribbons and Rosettes

9

ACCESSORY BOUTIQUE

Copy Designer Lampshades

Enjoy More—
& More Beautiful—Lighting

Wired-Edge "French" Ribbons

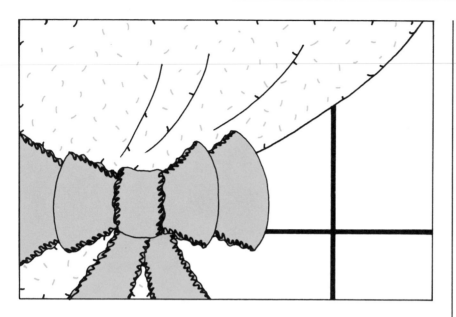

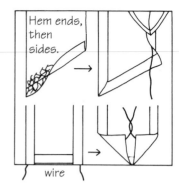

Transform fabric into intriguing, three-dimensional ribbons: Simply fuse or serge wire to the edges. Even the inexperienced can master these techniques and relish shaping formerly flat fabric into luscious bows and rosettes.

The Materials

• **Fabric:** Any light- to mid-weight. One yard of 45" (115cm)-wide fabric will yield 12 unfinished 3" by 45" (7.5cm by 115cm) crosswise strips or 15 unfinished 3" by 36" (7.5cm by 90cm) lengthwise strips. *For reversible ribbons:* Fuse two fabrics wrong sides together; then cut into strips, or serge two strips wrong sides together.

• **Wire:** A roll of any rust-proof stainless steel or brass wire—24- to 28-gauge beading wire for most light- to mid-weights, and heavier 20-gauge for most heavier fabrics. The smaller the gauge, the bigger the wire.

• **Thread for the serged method:** Any other decorative thread or combination of threads used in the upper looper of the 3-thread stitch or the looper of a 2-thread stitch—see page 75. All-purpose or serger thread can be used in the needle and looper.

• **Fusible-transfer web for the fused method:** 2-1/2 yards (2.3 meters) of 3/4" (2cm)-wide precut strips required for finishing 36" (90cm)-long strips; 3 yards (7.5cm) for 45" (115cm)-long strips.

• **Crummy scissors:** For cutting the wire. Spare your other scissors.

The Steps

1. Cut the fabric into strips the length and width desired. Allow at least 36" (90cm) in length if you will be tying a bow. *Optional:* Taper the ends. Decide whether to fuse or serge the short ends and proceed to the appropriate Step 2 below.

For fusing:

2. "Fast fuse" the short ends—see page 73. Repeat for the long edges, laying wire in the hem fold when fusing web-to-web. Allow 3" (7.5cm) wire extensions at each corner; trim or twist.

For serging:

2. Serge with balanced-tension rolled-edge serging or serge-finish the short ends.

3. Place the wire under the back of the foot and over the front of the foot, between the needle and the knives. Allow a 3" (7.5cm) tail behind the foot—start serging over the wire for 1" (2.5cm), continuing onto the fabric. Trim about 1/4" (6mm) off the fabric edge. Serge off the strip, staying on the wire for about 1" (2.5cm), and then off—angle the wire to the left. Allowing a 3" (7.5cm) tail, clip the wire and chain. Dab with seam sealant; allow to dry. Clip the tails.

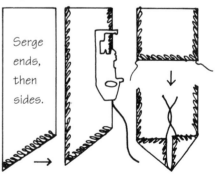

Optional for serging: Use a beading or cording foot to automatically guide the wire between the needle and knives.

Optional for fusing or serging: Allow 3" (7.5cm) wire tails and twist together to chevron the short ends. Trim or tuck under the wire.

Wonderful Wired-Edge Accents

Note: *All the accents shown here use basic wire-application how-to's featured on page 58.*

- *Wired edges, sewn.* Sewing's slower than serging or fusing, but easy nonetheless. *For edge finishing,* satin-stitch over the wire. A slotted foot is helpful. *For gathering,* zigzag-baste over the wire, holding the wire so the fabric ruffles behind the foot (or push the fabric in from both ends to gather).

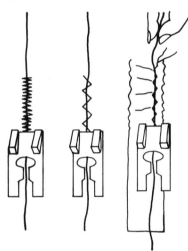

- *Florist-bow flourishes.* Twist wires to join; then twist the loop into a bow. Or form bow rings for floral ties—see page 14. Or loop into a classic florist bow, securing with wire.

florist bow

- *Bigger bows*—out of tapestry, for example. Make 6" (15cm)-wide or wider ribbon with wired edges. Wrap rather than tie into a bow. Hand-pleat a 4" to 8"-long (10cm to 20cm-long) wire-edged strip, and baste or glue over bow loops. Accent vases, wreaths, baskets, pictures, pillows, and window treatments.

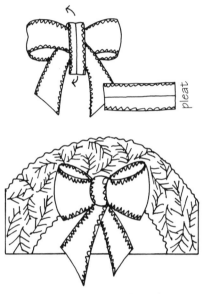

- *Picture bows.* Soften frame angles, or unify a group of pictures. Adorn with a simple bow. Hang the bow separately, from a soft-drink can tab. Hang the picture over the bow.

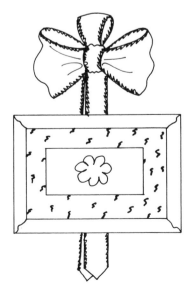

- *Wired rosettes.* Cut bias fabric strips 1" – 4" (2.5cm – 10cm) wide by 16" – 45" (41cm – 115cm) long. Taper the ends. Fuse, stitch, or serge wire to the straight edge. With the longest stitch possible, zigzag or serge wire to the tapered edge; hold the wire so the fabric ruffles behind the foot and/or push the fabric in from both ends to gather. Roll up into a rosette.

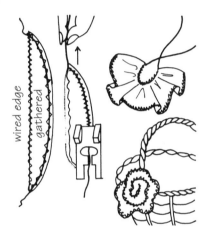

wired edge   gathered

- *Garland and tieback bows.* Scale up the width and length of the wired-edge ribbons, then tie creatively. Such fun!

Better-yardage-yield tip: Wrap bows with wire—see florist bow, left—rather than traditional tying.

Nearly-No-Sew Pleated Shades

Who would ever guess that pleated lampshades would be so easy to make? Just fuse and fold—there's no machine sewing required, only two rows of quick hand sewing.

The Materials

• *Fabric:* Tightly constructed light- to mid-weight fabrics, cottons or cotton blends. For most shades, from 2 to 2-1/2 yards (1.8 to 2.3 meters) will be required, unless the fabric is cut on the crosswise grain and pieced—see Step 2, below.

• *Nonwoven fusible backing:* Heavy, very crisp decorator stabilizers—see page 78. Yardage requirements will be the same as for the fabric. *Optional:* "Paperize" the fabric rather than use nonwoven backing—see page 65.

• *Fusible transfer-web strips:* About 5 yards (4.6 meters) or twice the fabric/cover length.

• *Cone-shaped shade frame or lampshade,* with or without cover intact. *Optional:* Spray-paint bare frames to match the fabric color.

• *Satin cording or ribbon:* 5 yards (4.6 meters) narrow enough to be hand-sewn through the shade—e.g., 1/8" to 3/8" (3mm to 1cm).

• *Thick craft glue*

• *Large-eyed tapestry needle*

• *Ruler, tracing wheel or pizza cutter, dull knife* for scoring.

The Steps

1. Calculate the fabric and backing dimensions required:

Top circumference X 5	=	_____
For extra fullness	+	20" (51cm)
Equals total length in inches (cm)	=	_____
Divide total length by 36" (100cm)	=	_____
for the requirement in yards (meters)		
Frame ring-to-ring height	=	_____
For hem allowances	+	2-1/2" (6.3cm)
Equals total depth	=	_____

2. Cut out the fabric and backing, with the length running parallel to the lengthwise grain. Trim 3/4" (2cm) off each long side of the backing. Center the backing on the fabric with 3/4" (2cm) hem allowances on each side. Fuse, following the manufacturer's

directions. "Square up" the stabilized fabric—each corner should be a right angle.

3. Use the transfer-web strips to fuse the full hem width to the backing—3/4" (2cm). Then mark and score the back of the shade every inch. For even edges, score precisely. Fold in accordion-style pleats, and wrap with scrap fabric. Let sit for a few hours to set the pleats.

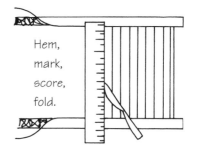

Hem, mark, score, fold.

4. Use a large-eyed needle to sew ribbon or fine satin cording through the pleats 1" (2.5cm) from the top and lower edges. Wrap around the frame, drawing up the pleats around the shade.

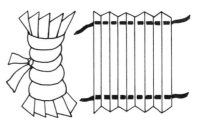

5. Overlap the last pleat and glue in place. Tie the cord or ribbon decoratively and trim the tails to the length desired. *Optional:* Hand sew the pleats to the top ring of the frame, as shown.

Goof-Proof Sewn & Glued Shade

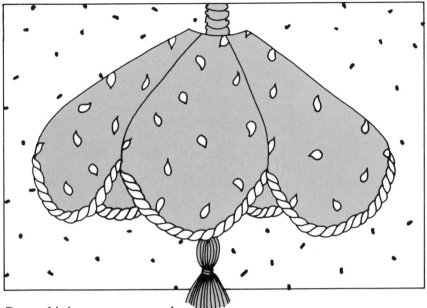

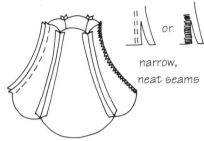

balanced stitch or double straight-stitch with two rows of stitching about 1/8"(3mm) apart.

narrow, neat seams

*By combining sewn or serged
seams and glued hems, I arrived at my favorite fast, fitted shademaking
method. The other essential ingredient in this goof-proof method mix is
stretch-to-fit bias fabric, which forgives any fitting inaccuracies.*

The Materials
• *Fabric:* Any tightly woven cotton or cotton blend. With the exception of extra-large frames, most require no more than 1 yard (.9 meter).
• *Shade frame:* Any frame with a convex (curving outward) shape. *Optional:* Spray paint the frame beige, or to match the shade fabric.
• *Glue:* One tube or bottle of any thick craft glue. *Important:* Use only permanent glues on vinyl-covered frames.
• *Optional: Decorative gimp* for finishing the wrong side of the upper and lower ring hems. For yardage, measure the lower edge and add 6" for fitting insurance. *Long, decorative-head pins,* for fitting the fabric shade. *Fringe, or other trim,* for the lower edge. *Tassel,* for the pull cord or switch. *Spray bottle,* for misting with water to shrink cotton or cotton-blend shades—test on scraps first.

The Steps
1. Cut out the shade pattern pieces on the bias—important for a taut fit and strong, ravel-free seams—see page 77 for how-to's.

2. Machine baste the fabric pieces right sides together, starting and stopping the seams 1-1/2" to 2" (4cm to 5cm) from each end. Try on the frame, checking for a tight, wrinkle-free fit. The seams should align with the ribs. Make any alterations necessary. I usually have to take in some or all of the seams at least slightly.

3. After the fitting is acceptable, resew the seams with a close stitch— 12 – 16/inch (12 – 16/2.5cm). Either serge with medium-width

4. Then stretch the shade over the frame and with long pins, secure along the upper and lower rings. Working section by section, upper ring to lower ring, lightly apply glue to the frame, then adhere fabric to the frame. Stretch the fabric tightly and keep the seams in line with the vertical ribs.

5. After the glue has dried completely, use small, sharp scissors to trim away the excess hem allowances. *Optional:* On the underside, glue gimp to cover the hem edges. Or glue fringe or trim to the inside or outside edges, and/or hang a tassel from the pull cord or switch. *To slightly shrink-fit the shade further,* mist lightly.

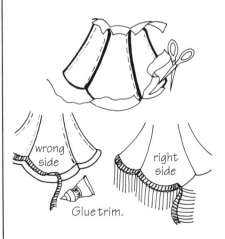

wrong side

right side

Glue trim.

More Lamp & Lampshade Makeovers

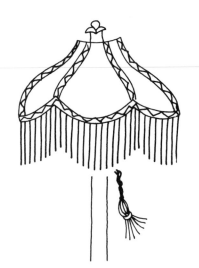

• **Practice trim tricks.** For the fastest shade transformation, glue gimp or fringe or any flexible braid, trim, or lace on a ready-made. This hides raveled edges or stains and coordinates two different but similar shades. Hang tassel accents on the switches.

• **"Scarf" a shade.** Cover hanging shades with a large, edge-finished square or with a round scarf or napkin—from 30" to 40" (76cm to 102cm) in diameter. Find the center and cut a slash large enough for the plug, finishing the edges with seam sealant. *Or drape a table lamp* with a square or round. Make sure the fabric is at least 3" (7.5cm) from the bulb.

• **Slipcover a shade.** Cut a rectangle 2 to 2-1/2 times the top-ring circumference by the height plus 3" (7.5cm). Seam into a circle. Fuse a 1" (2.5cm) lower-edge hem and press a 1" (2.5cm) top hem. Fuse or stitch shirring or smocking tape about 3/8" (1cm) from the top-edge fold. Draw up the cords to fit the frame or shade top, and tie. *Variation:* Substitute an elastic casing for the decorator tape.

decorator tape

• **Sock a base or cord.** Tie fabric around the lamp base, securing with ribbon or satin cord. *Or cover a cord:* Seam a tube twice the length of the cord, and wide enough to fit over the plug. Slide over the cord, shirring the fullness evenly.

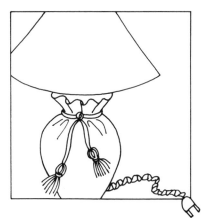

• **Frame + fabric = beautiful bowl.** Turn a half-moon frame upside-down and wrap with fabric, stuffing the excess inside. Makes a charming plant pot, snack-, or punch-bowl cradle. *Optional:* Accent with rosettes formed by pulling excess fabric through small *Infinity Rings*.

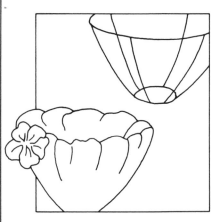

• **Pre-pleat shade fabric** for a drum-shaped or slightly flared shade. Use pleats—see page 70 and 80—and fuse to shade-backing material. Then cut out the shade pattern—see page 77, bind the edges—see page 74, lap, and glue.

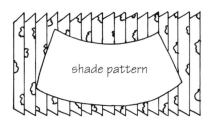

shade pattern

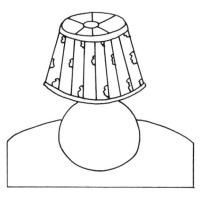

Give Budget-Wise, Beautiful Gifts

"Fabric" a Tree:
The Ornaments, Skirt, & Wrappings

10

INSTANT HOLIDAY
INSPIRATIONS

Make Innovative,
Salable Bazaar Items

Transform Your Home
for the Holidays

Bazaar Best Sellers & Great Gifts

• **Sell wire-edged ribbon** by the yard, plus matching bows—see pages 58 – 59. Inspire buyers by displaying ribbon-embellished wreaths, garlands, and gifts. Be prepared: Your customers will want to buy display items.

• **Wrap baked goodies with "foilized" fabric.** Substitute aluminum foil for paper when making "paperized" fabric—see page 65. Cotton fabric works best. Working from the fabric's right side, fuse the webbed side to the dull side of the foil. Then use the "foilized" fabric to wrap baked goodies, like fruit cake (does anyone really eat it?). Also top jars of yummy goods with rounds of foilized fabric, tied with a bow. *Caution:* Only the crummiest scissors qualify as foil-cutting tools.

fabric

web

foil

• **Wrap bottles of your special-recipe vinegars, ciders,** and other refreshments with a large napkin—20" (51cm) or more. A ready-to-go gift!

wrap & tie

• **Sell or give napkin creations.** At our recent church bazaar, we sold 400! Round napkins folded into tree shapes are always popular. Fuse, sew, or serge dozens. Make rings, too—see page 14. Sell in "fabricated boxes," shown at right. Or line a basket with a napkin. Fit the napkin lining by gathering together the center and securing with a rubber band; then flounce the edge. For more ideas, refer to *Quick Napkin Creations*—ordering information is on page 96.

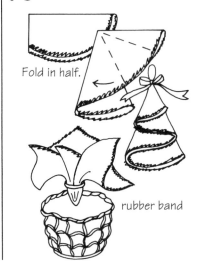

Fold in half.

rubber band

• **Decorate a small tree with your "irresistible ornaments"**—see page 65. Offer the featured ornaments for sale.

• **Fabricate boxes for your treasures.** Sandwich file-folder weight paper or extra-crisp nonwoven stabilizer between the wrong sides of transfer-webbed fabric—see page 70; fuse. Cut out a 12" (30cm) square or any size desired and finish the edges with pinking, trim, or serging. Stitch to miter the corners as shown. *Optional:* Trim off the corners, and turn the seams to the inside.

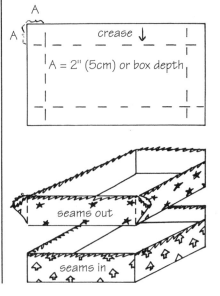

A

A

crease

A = 2" (5cm) or box depth

seams out

seams in

Irresistible Ornaments & Garlands

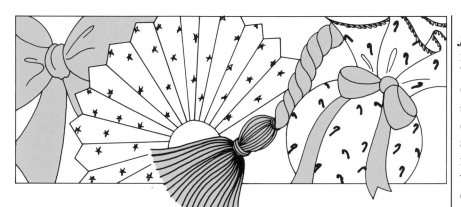

• "Paperize" fabric.

Create an exciting, ravel-resistant material that creases, curls, and folds. Fuse transfer web to the wrong side of your fabric. Then with little or no steam, fuse fabric to the wrong side of gift wrap—metallics are lovely.

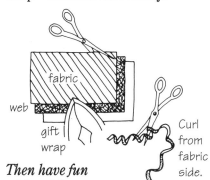

fabric
web
gift wrap
Curl from fabric side.

Then have fun with quick cut-ups.

Try a looped chain garland, or cut 5" – 8" (13cm – 20cm) circles and twist into cones. Fill with dried flowers and embellish. Make garland magic by accordion folding and cutting easily identifiable shapes.

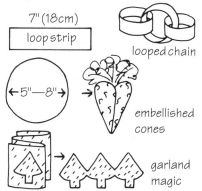

7" (18cm)
loop strip
looped chain
← 5"—8" →
embellished cones
garland magic

• Trim with tassels.

Hang tassels from wire ornament hangers, or adorn with ribbon bow-ties. For a garland, hang satin cording accented with tassels—secure with wire.

• Fabricate fabulous spheres.

Finish the edges of 13-1/2" (34cm)-diameter rounds or squares with pinking, fusing, or serging. Wrap over a 3" (7.5cm) *Styrofoam*® ball, securing at the top with a rubber band or wire. Embellish with curled gift-wrap ribbon, or satin cord and tassels.

Wrap styrofoam ball.

• Score a big hit with mini-fans.

Cut a paperized fabric rectangle, about 4" by 14" (10cm by 36cm), and square the corners. On a firm surface, score the paper side with a dull kitchen knife every 1/2" (1.3cm). Fold accordion-style. Hold the pleats by running a basting thread through the pleats 1/2" (1.3cm) from the edge and hand tacking the last pleats on each side together. Accent with brass buttons or bells handstitched or glued on. *Variation:* Using a pleater board to pleat—see page 80, handstitch together at one end and embellish.

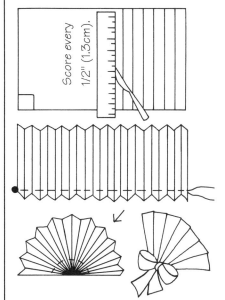

Score every 1/2" (1.3cm).

• Flourish with wired-edge bows and rosettes

—see pages 58 – 59. Make long ribbon strips any width, cut to length, and bow-tie. Attach rosettes with their gathering wire to tree boughs or wreaths.

Hurried Holiday Transformations

- **Staple a pin-up board to display holiday greetings.** To save space, cut the foamboard base to fit inside a picture or mirror frame. For how-to's, see "Make movable walls," on page 56.

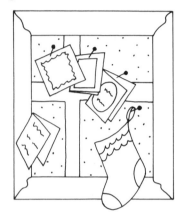

- **Swag with fabric.** Use long, 12"- to 30"-wide (30.5cm- to 76cm-wide) strips. The heavier the fabric, the narrower the strip. *Optional:* Edge-finishing by pinking, serging, or fusing. Fasten with rubber bands or swag holders to staircases or mantels, pulling fabric loops through to create rosettes and poufs.

- **Slipcover with holiday fabrics,** to add a festive look to any room—see page 44.

64" (160cm)

17" (44cm)

Square, hem, score, pleat.

wire

stands

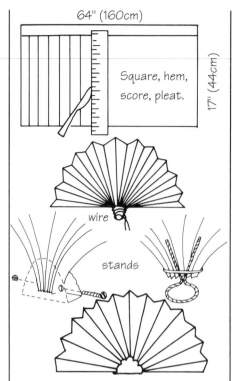

- **Fold a dramatic fan.** Cut as shown, out of paperized fabric—see page 65—or fabric stabilized with fusible shade backing—see page 60. Cut the paper or backing 1" (2.5cm) narrower than the webbed fabric, so that you can fuse a hem along one of the long sides. Score and fold every inch (2.5cm). With 28-gauge wire, wrap the pleats together about 1" (2.5cm) from the unhemmed side. If necessary, trim to even the wrapped edges.

   Glue on a large button, bow, or charm to cover the wire. Make a stand from a wire hanger, and insert through the wrapped wire. *Variation:* Stand upright with Repcon's *Fan Decor. Optional:* Increase stability by gluing mini-blind or ruler slats in the pleats that rest on the floor. *Perfect-pleat tip:* "Square up," making all corners right angles, before hemming, marking, and scoring—even every time!

- **"Fabric" a luxurious wreath or garland.** Using bases from Repcon, weave yards and yards of fabric through the spokes. Adorn with satin cord, trims, and dried flowers. Hang on a wall, on or over a door, from the ceiling, or use as a centerpiece.

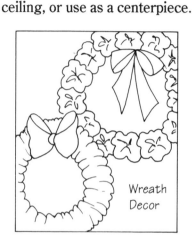

Wreath Decor

- **Create an instant "skirt"** by draping three or more yards of fabric under the tree. *Or make a 90" (229cm)-wide round tablecloth,* pieced down the middle. Stitch only to the center, leaving the rest of the seam open. *Utilize your fabric stash for gift wrap, too.* Wrap and rubber-band, or wrap and tie as shown for pillows on page 50. Trim with wire-edged ribbons—see page 59, satin cord, tassels, and curled paperized strips—see page 65.

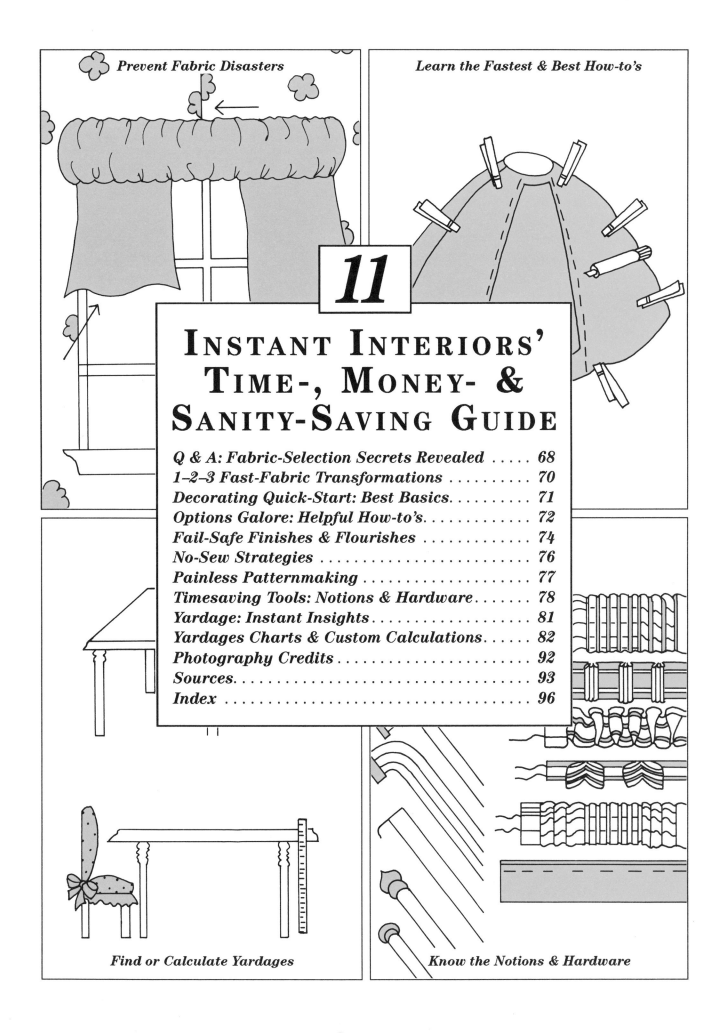

Prevent Fabric Disasters

Learn the Fastest & Best How-to's

11

INSTANT INTERIORS' TIME-, MONEY- & SANITY-SAVING GUIDE

Find or Calculate Yardages

Know the Notions & Hardware

Q & A: Fabric-Selection Secrets Revealed

When it comes to selecting fabric, don't be intimidated if you don't have a design degree. You know what you like—don't let outdated decorating dictates or those of your friends overrule your preferences. Create an environment that pleases you and your family, and remember: Interiors are never done, but always works-in-progress, continually evolving.

Do you really love the fabric(s)? Why waste your time or money on a fabric that is just OK? My hunch is that you will live with your choice, even if it's a temporary decorating solution, longer than you ever expect, so be sure you love the fabric.

Is the quality worthy of your precious time? Take my tried-and-true advice: *Buy better fabric.* Sorry—I realize that probably means *more expensive* fabric. Tightly constructed weaves, luscious colors, interesting textures, and well-designed prints camouflage less-than-expert techniques and elevate instant projects to custom-look status. In relation to the amount and length of use, fabrics chosen for decorating are a bargain at just about any price.

Can you afford the fabric or time that a major overhaul would require? If you're doubtful, why not start small? Make pillows—see pages 46 – 50—and continue to build your confidence and budget on this first success.

How will it look in the room? Test fabric in a room by draping a test yard on a window over a couch or chair. Rejects can be recycled into napkins—see page 14—and drawer linings—see page 56. Study the test fabric under both artificial and natural lighting. Also, consider the color/print scheme of the entire house or apartment, particularly if rooms open to each other. "Connector" prints or colors, used in both rooms, can tie together adjoining rooms. For those personal places—baths and bedrooms—pros tell me "do your own thing," not necessarily relating them in color or style to the rest of the house. I agree.

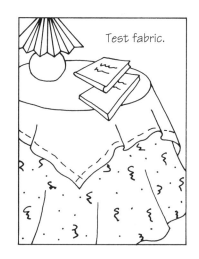
Test fabric.

• **Instant-selection solution:** *Overwhelmed by the fabric-selection process?* Start with an easy project, such as a tablecloth and topper in your statement print/solid and a filler. If you like the results, add coordinating projects. If you don't, give the set as a gift.

Are there coordinating prints and/or solids that could be combined in the room scheme? Decorating pros say that a guideline to follow is: A medium- to large-scale "statement" print for 60% of the room, mixed with two or more coordinated but usually different-scale "filler" or "enhancement" prints and solids in unequal proportions. For accessories, consider "accent" prints or solids. Try to avoid a too-matched, furniture-showroom look; be off a shade or two, and consider fabrics from more than one manufacturer. *Color-match tip:* When choosing coordinates, study the color key printed on the selvage of decorator fabrics.

Is the print overwhelmed or diminished by the project or in the room? On a cushion, the print should be scaled so that at least one entire motif fits on the top, whereas in a large room, small-scale prints can get lost. Gathers, pleats, and drapes can scale down any large-motif print, in effect creating a companion filler print out of the same fabric.

Consider scale.

Does the fabric have enough body or weight for the project? Simulate the shape and drape of the project with the prospective fabric. If you love the fabric, but it isn't beefy enough, see page 70.

Is the fabric opaque enough without a lining? Gathers, drapes, pleats, quilting, or backing material can enhance opacity—see page 70. If lining is needed, choose one the same or slightly lighter weight, with compatible care requirements.

Is the fabric tightly enough constructed to resist ravelling? If exposed edges demand ravel-proofing, and you don't have a serger, which seams and finishes simultaneously, finishing may be essential—see pages 72 – 73.

Is there enough yardage for your project? Buy more fabric than you think you'll need. In fact, I seldom buy less than ten yards—

I admit my house is big and slathered in fabric! Plus, I buy insurance yardage, for extra accessories, and to replace any damaged or misplaced items. For estimates, refer to the yardages provided on pages 77 and 81 to 91. Dye lots can vary from bolt to bolt, so I also buy all from one bolt, if possible. *The key to instant decorating is plentiful yardage,* which can be puddled, draped, swagged, and tied instead of being tediously fitted. For large-motif prints that necessitate matching, add extra yardage—see page 81.

Would wide-width fabrics or sheets require less piecing—or eliminate it all together? More than ever before, fabrics are now available in 72" (180cm), 90" (230cm), and even super-wide 120" (300cm) widths. Sheets are favorite wide-width "fabrics," too. Unless you're covering king-size furniture, piecing may be totally unnecessary. Also consider railroading, or running the fabric crosswise, so the width becomes the length of the project. Doing so offers obvious advantages when working with *sheers*—no seam show-through; *border prints*—continuity of the design; or *pucker-prone fabrics*—no seams to pucker.

Can preprinted cutouts save you time? Engineered to be cut and sewn into napkins, pillows, runners, tablecloths, quilt tops, and a myriad of decorating accessories, these fabrics drastically shorten both cutting out and construction. The sophistication and versatility of the current crop of cutouts may inspire you, even if you've shunned these cheaters before. Ask for the companion print and solid yardage.

Will decoratively finished edges eliminate hemming? Lots of laces and embroideries are sold with one or both selvage edges decoratively finished. Some

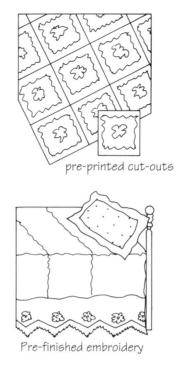
pre-printed cut-outs

Pre-finished embroidery

even provide openwork that serves as a rod casing. Not just for valances or café curtains, decoratively finished edges are quick to make into bed skirts and decorative ruffles, too.

Will the fabric resist fading? Vat-dyed fabrics usually cost more, but are also more colorfast. Untreated dark colors can be particularly susceptible to fading. Dry cleaning helps preserve the finish and color intensity of most fabrics.

How will the fiber content influence performance? It's hard to go wrong with all-purpose, tightly constructed cottons or cotton/synthetic blends. However, don't rule out *linen*—strong and elegant, but wrinkle-prone; *rayon*—wonderfully drapable but washability and body may be questionable; and *polyester*—easy care and affordable, but lacks absorbency and attracts static electricity.

Is washability a must? For longer-lasting sheen and body, I discourage prewashing of any fabric and too-frequent laundering

of washable ones. But let's face it: Laundering is essential for items like baby quilts, napkins, and everyday placemats. Between washings or dry cleaning, frequently vacuum pillows, curtains, upholstery, and quilts. Or try tumbling them or their covers in the dryer with a damp towel. You'll be shocked by the soil transferred to the towel. If you are tempted to wash a dry-clean-only fabric, I recommend washing a 12" by 12" (30cm by 30cm) remnant first. Then gauge the shrinkage and color or luster loss—e.g., chintz finishes cannot be renewed.

Has the fabric been treated with a surface dirt-, oil-, and water-repellant like Scotch-gard™, Tectron®, or Teflon®? If you live with active people, these finishes can minimize stains and launderings or dry cleaning—but not eliminate them, mind you. If the fabric isn't finished, or if it's been laundered, you can spray the project to minimize future laundering or dry cleaning.

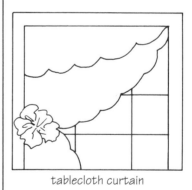
tablecloth curtain

Have you exhausted all possibilities? Break away from traditional fabric fare. Use lightweight rugs as upholstery or pillow fabric. Make curtains out of tablecloths, tablecloths out of sheets. Borrow brocades and satins for runners, pillows, even scarf valances. A friend of mine often decorates with garments. She even curtained windows with vintage bloomers—delightful!

1-2-3 Fast-Fabric Transformations

Decorating projects often call for fabric with more weight, body, stability, or finish. I've outlined many of my favorite fast-fabric transformation techniques here. Always test on scraps first. **Note:** *For specific brands and more product information, see pages 78 – 80.*

1. Fastest—About One Step

• **Fuse fusible-transfer web to the fabric.** For a heavier bond, use heavier fusible-transfer web.

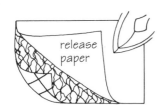

release paper

• **Fuse on fusible fleece** for an instantly "quilted" fabric. Press from the fabric right side. *Optional:* Add machine quilting— see *3. Fast* at right.

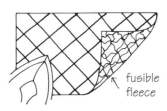

fusible fleece

• **Fuse on crisp, non-woven fusible stabilizers.**

• **Fuse fusible dressmaker interfacings** to add body to dress-weight fabrics used for decorating.

• **Apply stick-on shelf paper, self-adhesive fabric, or craft film to fabric.** If it's transparent, stick it to the right side; if it's opaque, stick it to the wrong side.

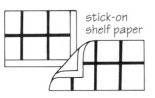

stick-on shelf paper

• **Spray on stain-repellant,** to protect untreated fabrics or to renew a finish.

• **Fuse a wired edge.** See page 59.

2. Faster—About Two Steps

• **Fuse two fabrics together.** Fuse transfer web to the wrong side of one fabric, remove the paper, and fuse to the wrong side of an unwebbed fabric. For more stiffness, use heavier web or fuse to another transfer-webbed fabric.

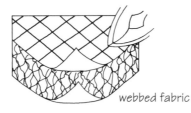

webbed fabric

Or fuse the transfer-webbed fabric to paper—anything from gift-wrap to cardboard— or foil. See pages 64 – 65.

Or sandwich a crisp nonwoven stabilizer or file-weight or heavier paper between the wrong sides of transfer-webbed fabrics. Fuse.

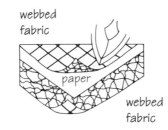

webbed fabric

paper

webbed fabric

• **Laminate with iron-ons.** Stick the sticky side on the right side of the fabric. From the fabric's wrong side, press with a dry, cotton setting, bonding the laminate.

• **Stiffen with spray-on, paint-on, or dip-in stiffeners.** Nice for accents like bows.

• **Piece strip patchwork** directly to batting. Lining is optional.

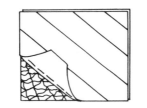

• **Serge a wired edge.** See page 59.

3. Fast—About Three Steps

• **Pleat the fabric.** Right side down, tuck into the louvers of a pleater board. Press. Fuse transfer-web or fusible tricot to the wrong side. Remove and cut to size. *Variation:* Allow 1" (2.5cm) beyond the pleater edges. Tuck in, right side up. Press. Machine baste allowances. Remove.

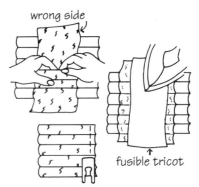

wrong side

fusible tricot

• **Quilt the fabric.**

Machine quilt. Place fusible batting, batting, or thin foam on the wrong side of the fabric; lining is optional. Fuse, safety-pin, or hand baste. From the right side, stitch through all layers.

"Tube-quilt." Stuff 4" – 5" (10cm – 13cm) channels with fiber fill or foam chips. Seam or bind to close the tube ends. See page 42.

Reversible-strip quilt. See page 35.

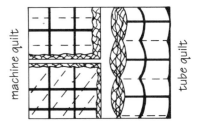

machine quilt

tube quilt

• **Shirr or pleat** to add weight, opacity, and body. Decorator tapes or machine attachments can speed the process.

• **Line the project** to enhance drape, body, and weight.

• **Satin-stitch a wired edge.** See page 58.

Decorating Quick-Start: Best Basics

If you don't read anything else in this chapter, read this page. Featured here are basics that will get you, disaster-free, through most projects.

● **Enlarge your work surface** to prevent pulling when sewing or pressing large projects.

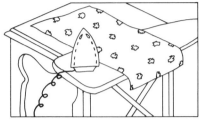

● **Piece odd numbers of lengths** to avoid a seam running through the center of a project. Plan for a full width in the center of the project, bordered by half-widths, which are lengths cut in half, lengthwise, or by full widths. *An exception:* Some prints and textures hide seams so well that a centered seam is inconspicuous.

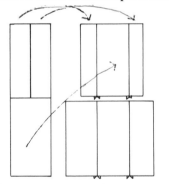

● **Allow extra yardage to match large-motif prints.** See page 81.

● **Consider railroading your fabric** to minimize matching, piecing, and yardage. See page 81.

● **Beautify corners by rounding them ever so slightly.** Whether you are seaming or finishing a corner, they look better and squarer.

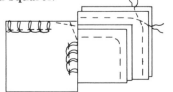

● **Work north-south, east-west,** for uniformity when hemming or edge-finishing squares or rectangles.

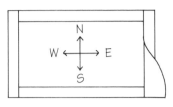

● **Round corners easily.** *For larger projects,* use a plate or large-pan lid. *For smaller projects,* use a saucer, cup, or a pocket-former template. Round corners together, or round one and use it as a pattern for the others.

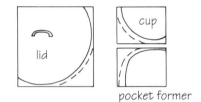

pocket former

● **Draw perfect circles** for round projects by rotating a measuring tape or string marked at half the diameter length. Half- or quarter-fold your fabric first, for speedier cutting.

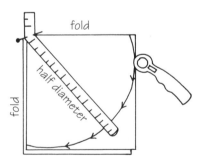

● **Estimate fullness ratios** when gathering, pleating, and shirring fabric. For sheers and lightweights, try 3:1; for mid-weights, try 2.5:1; and for heavy-weights, try 1.5:1 to 2:1. Also, some decorator tapes have a specified ratio. For instance, Gosling Tapes® are all conveniently 2.5:1. *An exception:* If you're short on fabric or want a flatter, more tailored look, decrease the ratio—i.e. 1.5:1.

● **Double-hem for better drape and less billowing.** If the hem is 4" (10cm), allow 8" (20cm). Press up 4" (10cm) twice and glue, fuse, or stitch in place—see page 72.

● **Avoid too-tight or too-roomy casings.** Measure the circumference of the rod, add 1/2" (1.3cm) ease for lightweights, 1" (2.5cm) for mid-weights, and 1-1/2" (4cm) for heavy-weights. Divide the number by 2, which equals the distance between the casing stitching lines, or the stitching line and the casing fold.

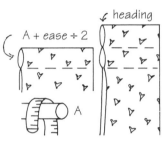

● **Make covers smaller than soft forms or fillers,** so that corners and edges will be filled out. If the filler is soft, such as a down comforter, the cover can be cut 1/2" (1.3cm) smaller or more on all sides. For soft pillow forms, cut the cover about 1/4" (6mm) smaller. For foam fillers, cut the cover to size, with no ease.

● **Think in threes for the best proportion:** three-swag valances, curtains tied back one-third or two-thirds the window height, three pillows across a wide bed, piecing in three sections.

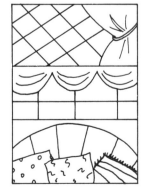

● **Improvise.** Do whatever works.

Options Galore: Helpful How-to's

Seaming Options

- **Fast-fused:** Press under the allowance. Fuse a strip of fusible-transfer web just inside the seamline. Remove the paper. Lap over the other side, aligning the seamlines. Fuse. Allow to cool completely. Check the bond; iron again, if necessary.

Fast-fusing tips: Follow the manufacturer's how-to's for iron settings. Also, consider using heavy-duty webs for heavier fabrics.

- **Easy-sew:** Straight-stitch and press open. Or lap and straight-stitch or zigzag the allowances together. *Optional:* Topstitch.

straight-stitched   lapped

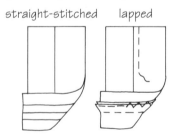

- **Serged:** Use a 3-, 3/4-, 4/2- or 5-thread stitch. Press the seam to one side. *Optional:* Straight-stitch the seam and finish the edges together or separately with 2- or 3-thread serging.

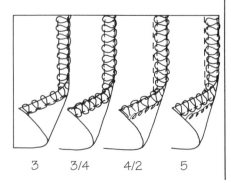

   3   3/4   4/2   5

Seaming Tips

- **Ravel-proof seam edges** with pinking—with or without staystitching—or use a fine line of seam sealant. Or finish with zig-zagging, regular or three-step, or serging. *Optional:* For additional stability, fuse down the allowance.

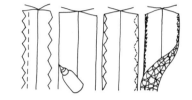

- **Wrap corners for perfect points.** After sewing or serging one side of the corner, wrap toward the other along the seamline. Then sew or serge the other side.

wrapped corners

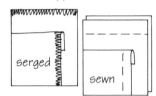

serged   sewn

- **Press seams open, before turning right sides out.** The pressed-open seam will be straighter and will align along an edge easily.

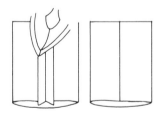

- **Trim off selvages if they pucker or pull the seamline.** Or release the puckering by clipping intermittently.

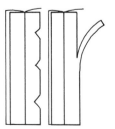

Hemming Options

Note: These how-to's are for double hems. Double hems are generally recommended for decorating—see page 71. Single hems may require edge finishing—see page 73.

- **Fast-fused:** Press the first fold of the hem. Press a strip of fusible-transfer web 1/4" (6mm) from the hem fold or edge. Peel off the release paper. Press up the hem again.

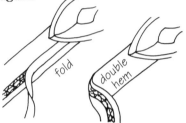

fold   double hem

- **Glued:** *For projects that will be laundered or dry-cleaned,* use permanent glue—check the label. *For all projects,* use thick or tacky glue. Run a bead of glue about 3/8" (1cm) from the hem edge. Air-dry briefly to increase tackiness. Finger-press; allow to dry completely.

double hem

- **Easy-sew:** Using invisible nylon thread and a long stitch, topstitch the hem from the right side. Or blindstitch by machine, using invisible or fine thread.

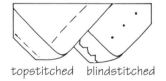

topstitched   blindstitched

- **Serged:** Using fine thread such as rayon, blindstitch the hem.

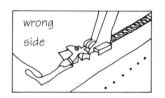

wrong side

Optional: Use a blindstitch foot or flatlock the hem. *For 3-thread flatlocking*, loosen the needle considerably, and tighten down the lower looper. *For 2-thread flatlocking*, loosen the needle only if necessary.

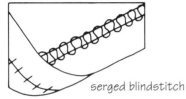

serged blindstitch

• **Blindstitched:** Use a special blindstitch machine, such as the *baby lock Blind Hemmer*.

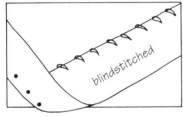

blindstitched

• **Decorative:** With one of your machine's decorative stitches, topstitch the hem. Or use a twin needle for straight or decorative stitching.

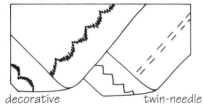

decorative   twin-needle

Edge-Finishing Options

• **Fast-fused edges:** Along the wrong sides of opposite edges, press strips of fusible-transfer web. *Optional:* Pink the edge, barely trimming the paper. Fuse half the hem width, web to web. Repeat for the remaining sides. *Variations:* Miter the corners. Or before fusing, sew or serge decoratively along the edges.

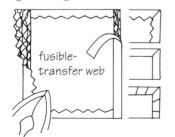

fusible-transfer web

• **Easy-sew edges:** 1) line to the edge; 2) twin-needle topstitch; 3) satin-stitch; 4) double satin-stitch —narrow first, then wider; 5) narrow double hem; or 6) decoratively machine stitch.

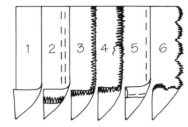

• **Serged:** 1) serge, turn, and topstitch; 2) work a narrow hem— rolled or balanced tension; or 3) decoratively serge-finish.

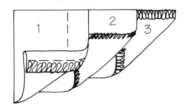

Edge-finishing Tips

• **Blend threads** to enhance color-matching, durability, accent, and coverage. Place the extra spools on an empty rod, in a cup, or on a coned thread stand. *When serging:* Use two threads in the loopers. *When sewing*, use two threads in the needle, increasing the needle size as necessary.

Mitering Options

• **Fast-fused miters:** Ravel-proof the edges. 1) Fuse up two opposite edges—see "Fast-fused hems," page 72. 2) Press up the remaining sides, folding in corner. 3) Fold in sides to miter corner. Repeat the fusing process, securing the miters and hems.

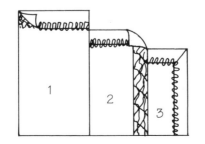

• **Fast-finished-and-stitched:** After all the edges have been finished and the hems pressed, simply topstitch.

folded miter

Fast-folded-miter tip: Fold in corner to form miters before fusing or stitching hems. Instant, stitchless miters!

• **Easy-sew miter:** Mark the hemlines. Fold the corners right sides together. Fold each corner again, aligning all raw edges. Using the diagonal foldline as a guide, straight stitch next to but not catching the fold; to avoid jamming, start 3/8" (1cm) in from the raw edges. Shorten the stitch to secure the seam ends. Trim the seam, finger-press open, and turn rightside out. Center the miter and repeat for the other corners. Turn hem under 3/8" (1cm), press, and topstitch or satin-stitch over the raw edge.

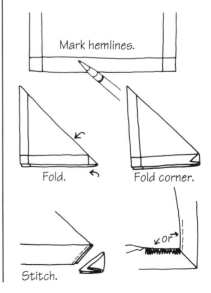

Mark hemlines.

Fold.   Fold corner.

Stitch.

Fail-Safe Finishes & Flourishes

● **Luscious "elastic" gathers:** Quarter-mark clear 1/4" (6mm) elastic and the fabric edge to be gathered. The total marked length should be the finished seam length. Sew with a long stitch over the elastic, just inside the seamline, stretching the elastic to match the quarter-marks. If necessary, increase density by simply pushing gathers closer together, or decrease by clipping the elastic to release stitches.

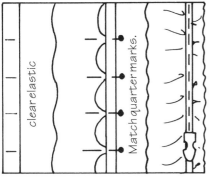

● **Goof-proof gathering thread:** Zigzag or serge over heavy thread, fine string, or dental floss. Feed thread through the slot or channel in the foot, if applicable on your machine. Wrap one end of the heavier thread around a pin and pull the other to gather.

Serged variations: For fine, controlled gathers, using a 3/4-thread stitch, feed the heavy thread between the right and left needle. Light-weight fabrics can be gathered with differential feeding set on 2 and a long stitch and/or by "finger tensioning," pushing or pulling the needle thread.

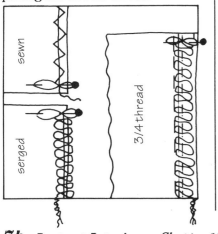

● **Fishing-line-flounced gathers:** Serge or satin-stitch over 12- to 40-weight fishing line. The bigger the number, the heavier the line. The steps are the same as for wired edges—see pages 58 – 59, with two *important* exceptions: Use stretchy fabric—bias or open-work wovens, knits, lace, tulle—and leave long tails about half the ruffle length at both ends. After applying, pull the edge to create the flouncing.

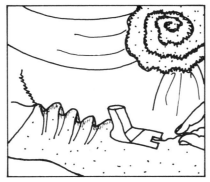

● **Ruffles—Pretty possibilities:** *Easiest:* Buy a ruffle strip with a self-gathering cord. *Reversible ruffles:* Self-line or line, seaming at the edge or decoratively serging. *Single-layer ruffles:* Finish the exposed edge—see page 73 for options. *Exposed ruffles:* Finish both edges, shirr 1/2" (1.3cm) from one long edge, and stitch over the shirring to apply.

Ruffle-muscle tip: Prevent wimpy corners by increasing gathering density at the point or curve.

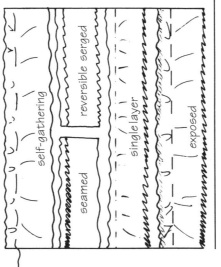

● **Best binding:** Buy wide bias hem facing or quilt binding. Or cut bias strips four to five times as wide as the finished binding. Piece on the straight of grain, and press under one long edge the same width as the finished binding. Stitch the right side of the strip to the wrong side of the edge; the seam width will be the binding width. Wrap, enclosing the edge, barely covering the first seamline. Edgestitch in place, close to the fold and over the first stitching.

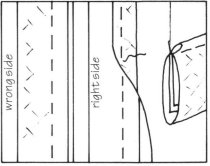

Sewn binding variation: Stitch the binding to the right side of the edge, wrap, and from the top side, stitch-in-the-ditch.

Serged binding variation: Serge-finish rather than fold under the exposed long edge. *Optional:* Use melt-adhesive thread, such as *ThreadFuse*™ or *Stitch 'n Fuse*, in the looper, eliminating the last stitching; wrap and press to secure the binding.

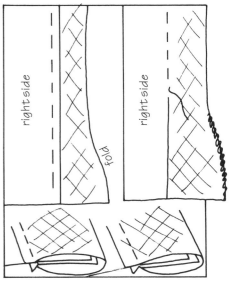

Terrific no-sew trimmings:
Fuse fusible-transfer web strips to the wrong side of trims, remove the paper, and fuse to the project. No more stitching indentations or puckering! If pressing is impossible, such as on lampshades, use tacky glue that's clear when dry. Apply to the trim; then position on the project.

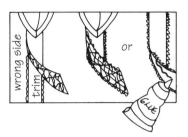

Fast, fabulous serged finishing: Play with a variety of stitch widths and lengths, tensions—balanced, rolled, or flatlocked, and thread types. Remember, the loopers are the most-exposed threads; try pearl cotton, topstitching thread, *Decor 6,* or braided flexible ribbon. For more in-depth how-to's, refer to my book, *Innovative Serging*—see ordering information on page 96.

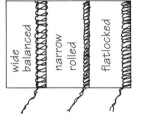

Or blend threads to increase thread coverage, color impact, and durability; use double strands in the loopers. Favorite "blends": Woolly stretch nylon with metallic and all-purpose or serger with rayon.

Variations: Add dimension by serging over filler, such as three to five strands of pearl cotton.

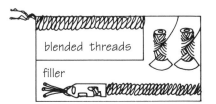

Perfect piping and welting:
Easiest: Purchase piping or satin cording with a lip or seam allowance.

Can't find cord with a lip? Using a zipper foot, blindstitch or zigzag the cord to bias hem facing.

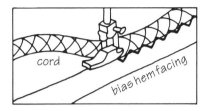

From scratch: Buy pliable cord in any diameter desired. Cut fabric strips the cord circumference plus 1" (2.5cm) for two seams. Cut on the bias for curves or on the straight grain for straight lines. Wrap the cord, and with a zipper foot, straight-stitch close to the cord.

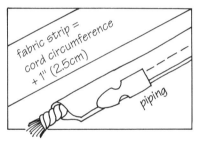

Piping-tool tip: Tube turners like *Fasturn®* can also insert cording or batting into piping—see page 80.

Welting (fat piping) variations:
1) Use fat filler cord or stuff with batting strips using a tube turner like *Fasturn®.* 2) Make fat filler by rolling 5" (13cm) strips of batting or fleece into 1" (2.5cm)-diameter tubes; glue. 3) Press fusible fleece on the wrong side of the strip, to the seamlines, as shown; fold and stitch.

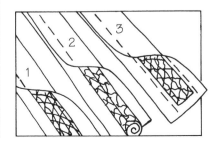

Ruched variation: Cut the fabric strips as described above, but twice as long as the cord. Secure the cord at one end. Every 6" (15cm) or so, raise the foot and pull the cord to gather the fabric.

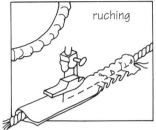

Perfect piping or welting applications: a pictorial review:

1. Use a zipper foot to apply, stitching along the seamline.

2. To seam, stitch directly over the first row of stitching.

3. Join narrow piping by tapering off and lapping. Heavier pipings can be butted and lapped. Or butt ends and wrap with a fabric or trim strip. Curves or corners? See page 47.

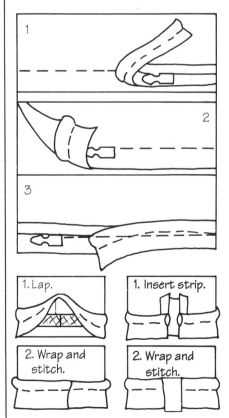

No-Sew Strategies

With apologies to my many friends who sell machines, here's how to avoid sewing altogether.

- **Take advantage of selvages or prefinished edges.** When piecing, arrange seaming so that the selvages are the outside edges, which can finish curtains, tablecloths, bed covers, and slipcovers. For ruffles and skirts, the selvage or decorative edge may also suffice as a finish.

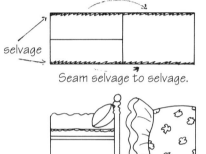

Seam selvage to selvage.

pre-finished edges

- **Pink to finish edges.** *Optional:* Fuse the pinked edge before laundering or cleaning. For a ravel-free finished edge, fuse the fabric to transfer-webbed fabric or paper, then pink.

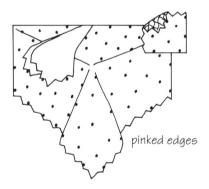

pinked edges

- **Staple fabric** to furniture—see pages 43 – 44 and 50; walls—see pages 54 – 56; and foamboard—see pages 38, 56, and 66.

- **Safety-pin**—see pages 37 – 38, 44, and 50.

- **Use ravel-free fabric** such as vinyls, laminates, synthetic suedes. Cut them out—you're done.

- **Rely on rubber bands.** Recycle fat bands; skinny ones can cut the fabric. *It's easy to hem:* Hand-pleat panels from the wrong side and rubber-band.

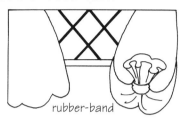

rubber-band

- **Rubber-band a rosette**—see page 28. Band a large 25" (68cm)-plus circle twice to create a choux.

- **Puddle hems for no-sew finish.** Allow at least 20" (51cm) for lavish puddling. Excess fabric stuffs itself for a fuller look. Puddle, hiding the raw edges. *Optional:* Rubber-band the hem edge of a panel before puddling—see illustration at top of column.

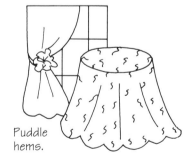

Puddle hems.

- **Glue hems and trims.** If washability or dry-cleanability is imperative, check the label. Test first on fabric scraps. Glue guns are terrific for adhering accents, but the adhesive may not last through washing or dry-cleaning.

- **Stick on hook and loop fasteners**—see page 79.

- **Fuse a seam or opening.** Press under the allowance, press the fusible transfer-web strip in place, lap over the other side, and fuse to seam—see page 72. Great for perfect matching!

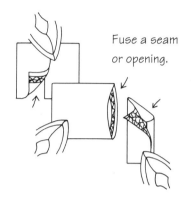

Fuse a seam or opening.

- **Fuse hems and edges**—see pages 72 and 73.

- **Fuse trims.** Fuse to the trim first, then to the project. New narrow fusible transfer-web strips make it fast and easy.

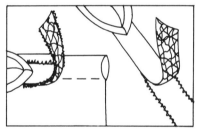

fusible-webbed trim

- **Fuse decorator tapes**—see pages 18 and 78—following the manufacturer's instructions. Just draw up the cords to shirr or pleat.

- **Fuse backings.** Craft backings are extra-crisp for decorating and crafts. Fusible fleeces "quilt" fabric without stitching. Fusible web not only bonds, but stabilizes and ravel-proofs, too—see page 78.

- **Fuse see-through lamination**—see pages 70 and 79.

- **Fuse iron-on hook and loop fasteners**—see page 79. *Remember,* one side can be fused; the other, stapled or glued.

Painless Patternmaking

Sewn & Glued Shade Patterns

(See page 61.)

1. With clothespins or long, large-headed pins, hold "pattern cloth" over three panels on the frame—see "Lampshade pattern cloth," page 79, or use tightly woven cotton scraps.

2. Outline the spokes of the center panel with a felt pen.

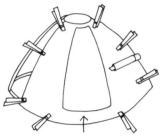

spoke outline

3. Remove the pattern cloth from the frame. Cut out the center panel, adding 1/2" (1.3cm) seams to the sides, and a 1" (2.5cm) hem to both the top and lower edges.

4. Mark the lengthwise grain on the pattern; fold this grainline to form a right angle. Mark the foldline—it will be the new straight of grain for the bias-cut panels sections.

Note: If you're re-covering a frame that has an existing cover that fits, use it as a pattern for the new shade, fine-tuning the fit—see Steps 3 and 4.

One-piece pattern tip: Roll any cone-shaped frame on pattern cloth, marking the circumference path; add for two seams—see page 62.

Sheet Dimensions

These dimensions are merely guidelines. Adapt to your fabric width, slightly narrowing the sheets as necessary to economize on fabric.

Flat Sheets

(Sewing how-to's on page 38.)

● *For standard sizes with 1" double hems on all sides, cut:*

Twin—70" by 108" (178cm by 275cm)
Extra-long Twin—70" by114" (178cm x 290cm)
Double—85" by 114" (216cm by 290cm)
Extra-long Double— 85" by 118" (216cm by 300cm)
Queen—94" by 114" (239cm by 290cm)
Extra-long Queen—94" by 118" (239cm by 300cm)
King—112" by 114" (285cm by 290cm)
California King—112" by 118" (285cm by 300cm)

Working opposite side to side, topstitch 1" (2.5cm) double hems throughout—see page 72.

Fabric- and time-saving tips: Eliminate lengthwise hems and let the selvages finish the edges. Also, there's no need to trim too-wide fabric—tuck extra width under the mattress.

Fitted Sheets
● *To convert flat to fitted:* Trim to the dimensions below.

● *To make fitted from fabric,* cut out these dimensions:

1. Mattress length + two mattress thicknesses + 4" (10cm) = *total unfinished length*

2. Mattress width + two mattress thicknesses + 4" (10cm) = *total unfinished width*

3. Corner cut out = *one mattress thickness + 2" (5cm)*

Cut out one corner; use it as a pattern for the other three. Sew as shown on page 38.

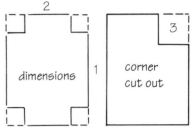

fitted sheets from fabric

Pillow Patterns

(See pages 36, 46 – 50.)

● *Seams: If using a medium to firm form,* add 1/2" (1.3cm) allowances to the outer edges. *If using a very soft form,* do not add seam allowances.

● *For zippered-back pillows:* Cut the top pattern in half vertically or diagonally, and add 3/4" (2cm) allowances.

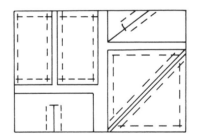

● *For sham-back pillows:* Cut the top-pillow pattern in half vertically, and add 4" (10cm) to one side of the back. Use this as a pattern to cut two backs. Refer to page 36 for construction steps.

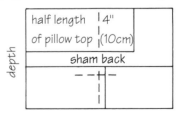

● *For pillow cases:* Cut a rectangle 35" long by 41" deep (89cm by 104cm). *For queen cases,* 39" by 41" (99cm by 104cm) and *for king cases,* 43" by 41" (109cm by 104cm). Hem and seam as shown on page 36.

Timesaving Tools: Notions & Hardware

Backings/stabilizers can be sew-in or fusible and nonwoven or woven. For the fastest stiffening of fabric, use a nonwoven, fusible stabilizer: *Craft-T-Back*™ by Dritz; *Decor-Bond*® and *Craft-Bond*® by Pellon; or *Crafter's Choice*™, *Fuse-A-Craft*™, and *Fuse-A-Shade*™ by HTC. Reserve sew-in nonwovens for projects sensitive to heat.

• *Better-beefier-fabric tip*: Dress-weight woven and nonwoven fusible interfacings can transform dress-weights into decorating-weights.

Batting and fleece add body, weight, loft, and insulation. Types include:

Bonded batting, which is lofty, with sizing on both sides, from 2 – 6 ounces, such as American Fiber's *Therma Quilt*, or Fairfield Processing's many *Poly-Fil*® battings.

Needle-punched fleece, which is a flatter, durable batting, such as *Armo*® *Fleece Plus*, *Dritz*® *Craf-T-Fleece*™ and *Big Fleece*™, HTC *Fleece*™, or *Pellon*® *Fleece*, *Quilter's Fleece*, and *Thermo-Lam*® *Plus*.

Fusible needle-punched fleece, which is a press-on variation, such as *Dritz*® *Fusible Craf-T-Fleece*™ and *Press-On Fleece*™, Fairfield's *Poly-fil*® *Traditional* and *Ultra-Loft*® *Needlepunched Battings*, HTC's *Fusible Fleece*™, and Pellon's *Fusible Fleece*™. Hobbs Bonded Fibers specializes in *Thermore*® and *Poly-down*® batting that is "beardless," meaning it won't creep through the fabric; *Poly-down DK*® is their new, grey batting for projects that are dark-colored. *Note:* Natural-fiber battings a priority? Look for cottons, such as *Warm & Natural Non-bearding Cotton Batting*, and wool.

• *Invisible-piecing tip:* To piece the batting, butt the edges of the batting and loosely hand catchstitch. Also, if possible, alternate piecing lines, layer to layer, to smooth out indentations.

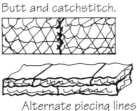
Butt and catchstitch.

Alternate piecing lines

Cornice-board kits, such as *Window Crowns by Beverly*, supply all the materials and how-to's needed.

Cutting tools (mats and rotary cutters) have made cutting easy.

Decorator tapes are easier to use than ever.

• *Don't-clip-the-cords-tip:* Wrap and knot in a figure eight or around a small piece of cardboard. That way, the fullness can be let out to press or launder flat.

Iron-on decorator tapes are fused, rather than sewn, to the project. In the home-sewing market, the most widely distributed are the new *Dritz*® *Iron-On*

Drapery Tapes, although Conso and Mastex iron-on tapes are also available.

Sew-on decorator tapes are stitched to the project; then the cords are pulled up to smock, shirr, or pleat the edge. Gosling is a bestselling brand; the tapes are made of lightweight polyester and are all conveniently designed for a 2.5:1 fullness ratio. Rhode Island Textiles's sew-on *Stitch 'n' Stretch* can often be substituted for shirring tape; draw up the elastic for a flexible fit.

• *Convert-sewn-to-iron-on tip:* Position 3/4" (2cm)-wide fusible-transfer web between the rows of cording to fuse Gosling's smocking tape in place.

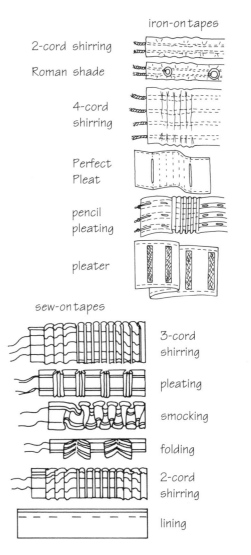

iron-on tapes

2-cord shirring

Roman shade

4-cord shirring

Perfect Pleat

pencil pleating

pleater

sew-on tapes

3-cord shirring

pleating

smocking

folding

2-cord shirring

lining

Fan hardware such as Repcon's *Fan Decor* secures the pleats, and holds it in an upright position.

Fiber fill is the polyester filling used for stuffing. Some manufacturers also offer their own brand of fiber fill, such as Fairfield's *Poly-fil*®.

Foam is a resilient foam-rubber filler that adds loft to projects. It's sold cut-to-size, by the sheet or slab, or as chips. If used for projects that will require cleaning, a removable cover is recommended. Cut sheets with shears; slice thicker slabs with an electric knife.

• *Better-foam-form tip:* To soften edges, wrap foam with fleece or thin batting before covering.

Foamboard (FoamCore) is a smooth, light-weight, foam-filled board sold in sheets by art- and office-suppliers—my #1 choice as a base for bulletin boards and movable walls.

Fusible-transfer web is a heat-activated, polyamide web with a release paper. Fuse to the wrong side of the fabric, remove the paper, and then fuse to another fabric, to paper, to foil, to wood, etc. Brands: *Dritz® Magic Fuse™*, HTC *Trans-Web™*, *Pellon® Wonder-Under®* (now in two weights—original and Heavy-Duty), and Therm O Web *HeatnBond™* (*Original* and *Lite*).

Fusible transfer-web strips are precut from 3/8" to 7/8" (1cm to 2.3cm) wide. For the fastest no-sew finishing, seaming, and hemming, keep these strips on hand.

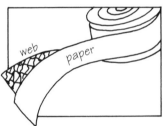

Some, such as *Dritz® Iron-On Hem-n-Trim™*, *Pellon's Heavy-Duty Wonder-Under® Transfer Fusing Web*, and Therm O Web's *HeatnBond™* (*Original)* have been formulated for mid- to heavy-weight fabrics and heavier-duty purposes. Other brands I use a lot include *HeatnBond™ Lite*, HTC's *Trans-Web™ Tape*, and Pellon's *Wonder-Under® Transfer Fusing Web*.

Fusible web is a heat-activated polyamide adhesive, sold by the yard or prepackaged, *without* the release paper. Popular brands: *Stitch Witchery®* and *Wonder-Web™*.

Garland, wreath, and frame hardware has been introduced by Repcon. Yards and yards of fabric can be poufed, rosetted, and draped from the spokes.

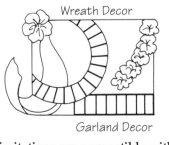

Wreath Decor

Garland Decor

Glue can secure trim, hems, and embellishments. Watch the labels for washability and dry-cleanability, making sure the care limitations are compatible with your project. Test all glues on fabric scraps, checking for discoloration, stiffness, bleeding, and durability.

Glue guns are plug-in tools that melt glue cartridges and are either manual- or trigger-fed. Glue guns are the ticket for permanently and instantly embellishing decor items that won't be washed or dry-cleaned, such as wreaths and tree ornaments. "Low-temperature-melt" models, much safer for use by kids, are now available.

Headboard kits, such as those from London Fabrics—see page 94, supply all the base materials and how-to's for making an upholstered headboard.

Hook-and-loop tapes such as *Velcro®*, and generic facsimiles, such as *Dritz Iron-on Hook & Loop Fastener Tape*, can be iron-on, sew-on, or stick-on. Great for fastening projects to mounting boards, window frames, furniture, and sinks.

Insulated interlining or composites such as The Green Pepper's *Aluminized Mylar Needlepunch* retains heat or cold, without bulk. For shades, consider *Warm Window™*, a four-layer channel-quilted composite.

Invisible nylon thread, now also available in the lighter #80 and .004 weights, for sewing and serging without changing thread color and for invisible topstitched hemming.

Iron-on laminates such as *Fab-Lam*, are now available. See "Stitches 'N Stuff" on page 95.

Lampshade frames can be salvaged from a worn or outdated shade, or purchased. If you have problems locating a frame, see pages 93 – 95. For exposed frames, spray paint to blend with the fabric.

Lampshade pattern cloth: HTC *Pattern-Ease™* and Pellon® *Stabilizers* (from light, #30, to heavy, #65) or *Tru-Grid®* are all viable options.

Mounting boards are usually 1" by 2" to 4" (2.5cm by 5cm to 10cm) fir or pine boards that are mounted inside or outside the window with "L" brackets. Flat curtains or shades can be stapled to the board *before* the board is installed for inside mounts or *after* for outside mounts. For lighter weight fabrics, inside-mounted "boards" can be cut from foamboard or heavy cardboard, and stapled or tacked in place.

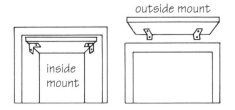

outside mount

inside mount

Pillow forms permit removal of the cover. Among the many I like are the 200-thread-count, cotton-covered *Poly-fil® Soft Touch* forms by Fairfield and the *Simplicity™ Percale Pillow Forms* by Air-Lite, although the cloth-covered forms are generally more expensive.

• *Fabricate-your-own-pillow-form tip:* Because fleece buffers and smooths the surface, serge or sew it seams out, stuff with fiberfill, and close the opening with machine stitching.

Pleater board is a stable, pleated cloth mat (now in three sizes) that make knife-pleating fabric fast and easy. See *Perfect Pleater* by Clotilde and *EZE-Pleater* by Lois Ericson. The pleated cloth is great for placemats, lampshades, or pillow accents. Tuck the fabric into the louvers, press, and sew or fuse—see page 70. The pleat width is doubled if every other louver is skipped, and tripled if two louvers are skipped. To piece, lap and fuse pleated sections. As a "take-up" gauge, 1 yard (.9 meter) of fabric yields 10" (25cm) of 1/4" (6cm) pleats, 17" (42cm) of 1/2" (1.3cm) pleats, 22" (55cm) of 3/4" (2cm) pleats, and 24" (60cm) of 1" (2.5cm) pleats.

Rings, plastic or brass, 1" – 2" (2.5cm – 5cm), are handy for securing tiebacks, rosettes, and poufs.

Rods for curtains, shades, and skirts are found in fabric, discount, and hardware stores, plus many catalogs. The casing size and look will reflect the rod type, size, and shape; choose accordingly. Remember, exposed rods can be painted, wrapped, or sleeved in fabric.

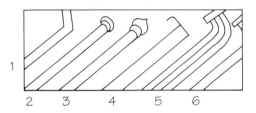

Shown left to right: 1) bent bay rod; 2) tension rod; 3) decorative wood rod; 4) wide continental or dauphine rod; 5) double rod; 6) single rod

• *Measuring tip:* For the complete width, include the rod "wraps," the curved ends that fasten to the wall.

Rubber bands can be recycled off newspapers for hemming, forming rosettes and poufs, or securing fabric. Avoid too-skinny bands—they can cut the fabric.

Safety pins are quick for securing tie-on pillow covers, skirts to beds, and slipcovers to furniture. Quilters' sizes, 1" (2.5cm) plus, are the most versatile.

Seam sealant is a clear liquid, that upon drying, finishes edges to minimize ravelling of threads and fabric fibers. Brands currently on the market: *Aleene's Stop Fraying™, Dritz® Fray Check™,* and Plaid's *No-Fray™.*

Shade-backing material stiffens and stabilizes fabric for roller shades or lampshades. Brands you'll find: *Dritz® Shade Maker™,* HTC *Fuse-A-Shade™,* and Pellon's new light-blocking *Wonder-Shade™.*

Specialty threads are built for strength, plus resistance to sun and abrasion, such as Coats' new *Upholstery & Home Dec Thread* and *Dritz® Upholstery Thread.*

Staplers or "tackers" are handy for hanging curtains, tacking fabric to chair seats and bases, making no-sew cushions, fabricing walls, creating no-sew bulletin boards, and making portable "walls." Light-duty staplers work well for most projects, although for fabric-track applications, heavier-duty electric staplers are suggested.

Swag holders offer a wide array of ways to hold fabric for window treatments, headboards, pillows, and much more. Brands you'll see: Claesson, Graber, and Kirsch. Only the *Infinity Ring* sold by Repcon is free-standing. Also, other accessories can double as holders: holdbacks (tieback hardware), small wreaths, towel hangers, and even picture frames.

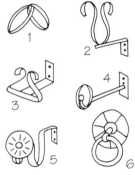

Shown right: 1) Infinity Ring (Repcon); 2) Magic (Claesson); 3) Tulip (Kirsch); 4) Spiral (Claesson); 5) Double Elegance (Claesson); 6) decorative ring (generic)

Track systems are the newest "fabricing" tools. *Quik Trak®* and *Craft Trak™* is sold in fabric stores and departments; *Quik Tex™* is the fire-rated version sold through designers.

Turning tools are designed to make turning fabric tubes and filling them with batting or cording effortless. The Crowning Touch's *Fasturn®*—see page 93—is one of the best known. Make trim, napkin rings, curtain tiebacks, and piping, fast.

Upholsterer's tapes are cardboard strips, sold in lengths or rolls, used for straightening edges when stapling, tacking, or mounting window treatments.

Zippers are essential elements in removable covers for comforters, pillows, and cushions. For extra-long lengths, look for zippers-by-the-yard, such as those by YKK and *Create A Zipper.*

Yardage: Instant Insights

Not knowing the answer to "How much fabric will it take?" can be a major obstacle to do-it-yourself decorating. I hope I can help. Throughout the book, yardages are given for popular widths and project sizes. In this section, additional yardages for all fabric widths and flat sheets, as well as custom-calculation formulas, are featured.

• ***Follow my one-and-only decorating rule:*** *Buy more fabric than you think you'll need.* I have never regretted adding 20% more.

• ***Note that fabric requirements are provided for both imperial and metric systems***, in recognition of my readers worldwide.

• ***Consider that all estimates have been rounded up slightly.*** Hence, you may make do with slightly less—but please see my first tip.

• ***Scrutinize yardage requirements.*** You may decide to narrow the project slightly, decreasing the number of lengths by one. Also, your total costs may be less using a more expensive, but higher-yield wide-width fabric.

• ***Utilize the charts as calculation insurance.*** If all your measurements are the same as mine, use the chart yardage. Otherwise, custom-calculate, then double-check by comparing your results to the closest size on the chart.

• ***Remember, multiples make sense.*** Yardages are given for one project. But your yardage may yield multiples, decreasing the cost per project.

• ***Determine whether or not your print should be matched.*** Don't do it unless an extra-large motif or plaid demands it. If the project is gathered or pleated, matching is not as critical.

• ***If the print does justify matching, allow extra yardage.*** Measure the repeat; add this to each length required. For instance, if each length required is 72" (180cm) and the repeat is 12" (cm), then increase each length to 84" (214cm). Plot the lengths and matching *before cutting. To match perfectly,* use the first length cut as a template for all the others.

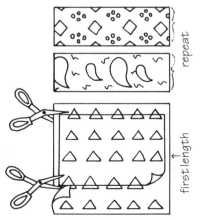

• ***Watch for automatic pattern match.*** Most decorator prints match automatically along the inside-edge of the selvage. If not, then the usable width is actually narrower than the fabric width. If so, use the usable width when calculating the yardage required.

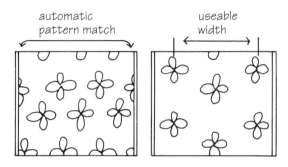

automatic pattern match   useable width

• ***Measure the actual width of your fabric.*** Often it is wider than labeled. That's good news: Your yardage requirements may decrease.

• ***Railroad fabrics to minimize yardage and piecing.*** Simply cut the total length required parallel to the fabric width. Worried about the print direction? Drape a sample piece, railroad-style, to test.

railroading: fabric width = project length

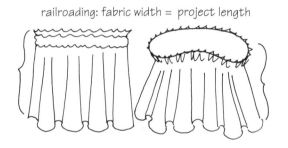

• ***Find sheet requirements here, too.*** Need to custom calculate? Standard ready-made widths and lengths for flat sheets are:

Twin—66" by 104" (168cm by 258cm)
Twin extra-long—66" by 110" (168cm by 279cm)
Double—81" by 110" (206cm by 279cm)
Double extra-long—81" by 114" (206cm by 290cm)
Queen—90" by 110" (230cm by 279cm)
Queen extra-long—90" by 114" (230cm by 290cm)
King—108" by 110" (275cm by 279cm)
California King—108" by 114" (275cm by 290cm)

Price- and size-wise, queen sheets are your best bet. Keep in mind that sheet sizes vary, so, for accuracy, measure both length and width. For the maximum yield, let the hems and borders out, and/or cut the project width parallel with the sheet length.

• ***Don't forget to add extra length for extras:*** *At least* 20" (51cm) in length for each puddled hem, knot, rosette, flounce, or bishop sleeve.

Table Toppings:
Yardage Estimates for Popular Shapes and Sizes

Square & Rectangular Tablecloths (1-1/2" hems allowed): Imperial

Table Size	Drop	36"	#L	45"	#L	54"	#L	60"	#L	72"	#L	90"	#L	120"	#L	Flat Sheets
34W x 34L	10	3-1/4	2	3-1/4	2	3-1/4*	2	1-5/8	1	1-5/8	1	1-5/8	1	1-5/8	1	1 Twin
40W x 60L	10	4-2/3	2	4-2/3	2	4-2/3	2	4-2/3*	2	2-1/3	1	2-1/3	1	2-1/3	1	1 Double
40W x 60L	16	8	3	5-1/2	2	5-1/2	2	5-1/2	2	5-1/2*	2	2-3/4	1	2-3/4	1	1 Double
40W x 90L	10	6-1/2	2	6-1/2	2	6-1/2	2	6-1/2	2	3-1/4	1	3-1/4	1	3-1/4	1	1 Double

Square & Rectangular Tablecloths (5cm hems allowed): Metric

Table Size	Drop	90cm	#L	115cm	#L	40cm	#L	150cm	#L	180cm	#L	230cm	#L	300cm	#L	Flat Sheets
86W x 86L	25	3	2	3	2	3*	2	1.5	1	1.5	1	1.5	1	1.5	1	1 Twin
102W x 150L	25	4.3	2	4.3	2	4.3	2	4.3	2	2.1	1	2.1	1	2.1	1	1 Double
102W x 150L	41	7.35	3	5	2	5	2	5	2	5*	2	2.5	1	2.5	1	1 Double
106W x 240L	25	5.9	2	5.9	2	5.9	2	5.9	2	3	1	3	1	3	1	1 Double

Round Tablecloths (1" hem allowed): Imperial

Table Size	Drop	36"	#L	45"	#L	54"	#L	60"	#L	72"	#L	90"	#L	120"	#L	Flat Sheets
30-diameter	10	3	2	3	2	1-1/2	1	1-1/2	1	1-1/2	1	1-1/2	1	1-1/2	1	1 Twin
30-diameter	29	7-1/2	3	5	2	5	2	5	2	5	2	2-1/2	1	2-1/2	1	1 Queen
42-diameter	10	3-3/4	2	3-3/4	2	3-3/4	2	3-3/4	2	1-7/8	1	1-7/8	1	1-7/8	1	1 Twin
42-diameter	29	8-1/2	3	8-1/2	3	5-3/4	2	5-3/4	2	5-3/4	2	5-3/4	2	2-7/8	1	1 King

Round Tablecloths (2.5cm hem allowed): Metric

Table Size	Drop	90cm	#L	115cm	#L	140cm	#L	150cm	#L	180cm	#L	230cm	#L	300cm	#L	Flat Sheets
76 diameter	25	2.8	2	2.8	2	1.4	1	1.4	1	1.4	1	1.4	1	1.4	1	1 Twin
76 diameter	25	6.9	3	4.6	2	4.6	2	4.6	2	4.6	2	1.4	1	1.4	1	1 Queen
107 diameter	25	3.5	2	3.5	2	3.5	2	3.5	2	1.7	1	1.7	1	1.7	1	1 Twin
107 diameter	74	7.8	3	7.8	3	5.3	2	5.3	2	5.3	2	5.3	2	2.6	1	1 King

Oval Tablecloths (1" hem allowed): Imperial

Table Size	Drop	36"	#L	45"	#L	54"	#L	60"	#L	72"	#L	90"	#L	120"	#L	Flat Sheets
30W x 48L	10	4	2	4*	2	2	1	2	1	2	1	2	1	2	1	1 Twin
40W x 60L	10	4-1/2	2	4-1/2	2	4-1/2	2	4-1/2*	2	2-1/4	1	2-1/4	1	2-1/4	1	1 Twin
40W x 60L	16	7-7/8*	3	5-1/4	2	5-1/4	2	5-1/4	2	5-1/4*	2	2-5/8	1	2-5/8	1	1 Double
48W x 72L	10	5-1/4	2	5-1/4	2	5-1/4	2	5-1/4	2	2-5/8	1	2-5/8	1	2-5/8	1	1 Double

Oval Tablecloths (2.5cm hem allowed)

Table Size	Drop	90cm	#L	115cm	#L	140cm	#L	150cm	#L	180cm	#L	230cm	#L	300cm	#L	Flat Sheets
76W x 122L	25	3.7	2	3.7*	2	1.8	2	1.8	2	1.8	1	1.8	1	1.8	1	1 Twin
102W x 150L	25	4.2	2	4.2	2	4.2	2	4.2*	2	2.1	1	2.1	1	2.1	1	1 Twin
102W x 150L	41	7.2*	3	4.8	2	4.8	2	4.8	2	4.8*	2	2.4	1	2.4	1	1 Double
122W x 180L	25	4.8	2	4.8	2	4.8	2	4.8	2	2.4	1	2.4	1	2.4	1	1 Twin

Yardages are estimated for solid colors only. Additional yardages will be required for matching large-motif prints.
All requirements are based on project length running parallel to the fabric or sheet length; cut crosswise if desirable and necessary to economize—see page 81. Consider cutting the project crosswise, particularly if using sheets or wide-width fabric.
*You may choose to make a slightly narrower cloth (decrease by one length) to economize on fabric or sheets.

Table Toppings: Quick Yardage Calculations

Note: Refer to "Table Toppings," pages 7 – 14.

- **Measure the length and width of the table top.**

- **Determine the desired drop**—the amount that hangs down from the edge of the table.

    Casual cloths—10" – 12" (25cm – 30.5cm) drops or about 1" – 2" (2.5cm – 5cm) above the chair seat.
    Formal cloths—16" – 24" (41cm – 61cm) drops
    Full-length cloth—reach the floor, about 29" – 30" long (74cm – 76cm). Add an extra 40" (102cm) to both the length and width for the puddled look.

- **Determine if the print requires matching**— see page 81. If so, you will need to add one print repeat to the length calculation—see Step 1, below.

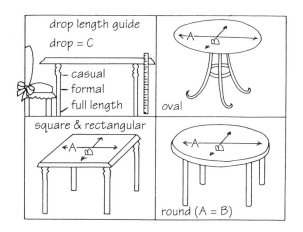

1. Calculate the total length required: **Add**

Table length (A)   ____

Drop times two (C X 2)   +____

Hem allowances   +____

    2" (5cm) total—rounds/ovals
    3" (7.5cm) total—squares/rectangles

Optional: One print repeat   +____

Total length required   =____

2. Calculate total width required: **Add**

Table width (B)   ____

Drop times two (C X 2)   +____

Hem allowances   +____

    2" (5cm) total—rounds/ovals
    3" (7.5cm) total—squares/rectangles

Seam allowances—   +____

    1" for each piecing line
    —if uncertain, add 2" (5cm)

Total width required   =____

3. Calculate the number of fabric lengths required:

Total width required—see page 81   ____

Divided by the usable fabric width   ____

Rounded up to the next whole number   =____

Total number of fabric lengths required = ____

4. Calculate total inches (cms) required:

Total number of fabric lengths   ____

Multiplied by the total length required   X____

Total inches (centimeters) required   =____

5. Calculate total yards (meters) required:

The total inches (centimeters)   ____

Divided by 36" (100cm)   =____

Total yards (meters) required   =____

More Table-Toppings Yardages & Tips

- **For one square or round topper:**

1 yard (.9 meter) of 36" (90cm)-wide fabric

1-1/4 yards (1.1 meters) of 45" (115cm)-wide fabric

1-1/2 yards (1.4 meters) of 54" (140cm)-wide fabric

1-3/4 yards (1.6 meters) of 60" (150cm)-wide fabric

- **For one 20" (51cm) wide, unfinished runner, cut crosswise, and pieced in the center—see page 13:**

1-1/8 yard (1 meter) of 45" (115cm)-wide fabric— yields up to 90" (230cm) in length. If you prefer no piecing, the unfinished runner length will be the yardage required.

- **For four or six placemats (multiply for larger quantities):**

1 yard (.9 meter) of 45" (115cm)-wide fabric—four 16-1/2" by 22-1/2" (42cm by 57cm) unfinished mats.

1 yard (.9 meter) of 45" (115cm)-width—six 13" by 17" (33cm by 43cm) unfinished mats.

- **For six napkins (multiply for larger quantities):**

7/8 yard (.8 meter) of 45" (115cm)-width—six 15" (38cm) square, unfinished napkins.

1 yard (.9 meter) of 54" (140cm)-width—six 18" (46cm) square, unfinished napkins. Extensive yardage charts and maximum yield tips are included in my book *Quick Napkin Creations*—see page 92.

Curtains, Shades, & Scarves: Yardage Estimates for Popular Sizes

Shirred Curtains (One panel, 2:1 fullness ratio, 6" hem/4" casing allowances): Imperial

Window Area	36"	#L	45"	#L	54"	#L	60"	#L	72"	#L	90"	#L	120"	#L	Flat Sheets
38W x 26L	2	2	2	2	1	1	1	1	1	1	1	1	1	1	1 Twin
38W x 62L	4	2	4	2	2	1	2	1	2	1	2	1	2	1	1 Twin
50W x 62L	4	2	4	2	4	2	4	2	2	1	2	1	2	1	1 Twin
62W x 74L	4-3/4	2	4-3/4	2	4-3/4	2	4-3/4	2	2-1/3	1	2-1/3	1	2-1/3	1	1 Double

Shirred Curtains (One panel, 2:1 fullness ratio, 15cm hem/10cm casing allowances): Metric

Window Area	90cm	#L	115cm	#L	140cm	#L	150cm	#L	180cm	#L	230cm	#L	300cm	#L	Flat Sheets
96W x 66L	1.8	2	1.8	2	.9	1	.9	1	.9	1	.9	1	.9	1	1 Twin
96W x 157L	3.7	2	3.7	2	1.8	2	1.8	1	1.8	1	1.8	1	1.8	1	1 Twin
127W x 157L	3.7	2	3.7	2	3.7	2	3.7	2	1.8	1	1.8	1	1.8	1	1 Twin
157W x 188L	4.3	2	4.3	2	4.3	2	4.3	2	2.2	1	2.2	1	2.2	1	1 Double

Roller Shades (2" side hem/trim allowances, 12" roll/length allowance): Imperial

Window Size	All Fabric Widths	Flat Sheets
24W x 30L	1-1/4	1 Twin
30W x 36L	1-1/3	1 Twin
30W x 48L	1-3/4	1 Twin
36W x 60L	2 (36" wide fabrics not wide enough)	1 Twin

Roller Shades (5cm side hem/trim allowances, 30cm roll/length allowance): Metric

Window Size	All Fabric Widths	Flat Sheets
61W x 76L	1.1	1 Twin
76W x 90L	1.2	1 Twin
76W x 122L	1.6	1 Twin
90W x 150L	1.8 (90cm-wide fabrics not wide enough)	1 Twin

Window Scarves (length allowances—36" for draping, 18" ease, two 8" hems): Imperial

Window/Area	Unfinished Length	All Fabric Widths (115cm+ recommended)	Flat Sheets
24W x 36L	158	4-1/2	1 King
36W x 36L	170	4-3/4	1 King
36W x 60L	218	6-1/8	1 King
48W x 72L	254	7-1/8	1 King, 1 Twin

Window Scarves (length allowances—90cm for draping, 45cm ease, two 20cm hems)

Window/Area	Unfinished Length	All Fabric Widths (115cm+ recommended)	Flat Sheets
61W x 90L	400	4.1	1 King
90W x 90L	430	4.3	1 King
90W x 150L	554	6.3	1 King
122W x 180L	645	5.6	1 King, 1 Twin

Yardages are estimated for solid colors only. Additional yardages will be required for matching large-motif prints.
All requirements are based on project length running parallel to the fabric or sheet length; cut crosswise if desirable and necessary to economize—see page 81. Consider cutting the project crosswise, particularly if using sheets or wide-width fabric.

Curtains, Shades, & Scarves: Yardage Calculations

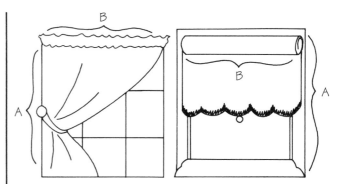

Note: Refer to "Quickest Curtains," pages 15 – 20, "Super-Simple Roller Shades," pages 22 – 23, and "No-Sew or Nearly No-Sew Scarves," pages 28 – 29.

Shirred (One-Piece) Curtain

• *Determine if the print requires matching*—see page 81. If so, you will need to add one print repeat to the length calculation (see Step 1, below).

Notes: For maximum light when the window is open, extend the rod to allow the curtain to stack beyond the glass. For divided curtains, see page 17.

1. Calculate total length required: Add

Height of the area to be covered (A)	____
Hem allowance—6" (15cm)	+____
Top casing allowance plus 1/2" (1.3cm) —if uncertain, add 3" (7.5cm)—see page 71	____
Top ruffle times 2—see page 26	+____
Optional: One print repeat	____
Total length required	=____

2. Calculate total width required: Add

Width of the area to be covered (B)	+____
Width (B) times fullness factor	+____

   For light-weights, 2.5 – 3
   For mid-weights, 2
   For heavy-weights, 1.5 – 2

Hem allowances—4" (10cm)	+____
Total width required	=____

3. Calculate number of fabric lengths required: Add

Total width required—see page 81	____
Divided by the usable fabric width	____
Rounded up to the next whole number	=____
Total number of fabric lengths required	=____

4. Calculate total inches (cms) required: Add

Total number of lengths	____
Multiply by the total length required	____
Total inches (centimeters) required	=____

5. Calculate total yards (meters) required:

The total inches (centimeters)	____
Divided by 36" (100cm)	=____
Total yards (meters) required	=____

Roller Shade

1. Calculate total length required: Add

Height of area to be covered (A)	____
Roll-up/hem allowance—12" (30cm)	+____
Total length required	=____

This will also be the total yardage/meterage requirement, unless the fabric or backing width is narrower than the window. If so, see Step 2 below.

2. Calculate total width required: Add

Width of area to be covered (B)	____
Side hem/trim allowances—2" (5cm)	+____
Total width required	=____

Note: If the fabric width is less than the total width required, railroad the fabric—see pages 23 and 81—multiply the total width required times two for the total inches (cms) required, and proceed to Step 3.

3. Calculate total yards (meters) required:

The total length required	____
Divided by 36" (100cm)	=____
Total yards (meters) required	=____

Window-Scarf Yardage Tips

• Hang the holders, rod, or mounting board first. After simulating the scarf drape with a long measuring tape, add 18" – 36" (46cm – 90cm) for each small to large bishop sleeve, bow, rosette or knot, 20" (51cm) for each hem puddle, and 54" (140cm) for each fan/flounce—see pages 28 – 29. Then, add another yard (meter) to the length—better too long than too short.

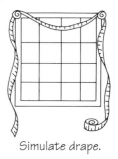

Simulate drape.

Bed Covers:
Yardage Estimates for Popular Styles and Sizes

Throw Bed Covers (20" drop, 2" double hems allowed): Imperial

Bed	Finished Size	36"	#L	45"	#L	54"	#L	60"	#L	72"	#L	90"	#L	120"	#L	Approx. Trim Meas.**
T	79W x 113L	10	3	6-5/8	2	6-5/8	2	6-5/8	2	6-5/8*	2	3-1/3	1	3-1/3	1	8-1/2
D	96W x 118L	10-1/4	3	10-1/4	3	10-1/4*	3	6-3/4	2	6-3/4	2	6-3/4	2	3-1/2	1	9-1/4
Q	102W x 118L	10-1/4	3	10-1/4	3	7	2	7	2	7	2	7	2	3-1/2	1	9-1/2
K	120W x 118L	13-7/8	4	10-1/4	3	10-1/4	3	10-1/4*	3	7	2	7	2	7*	2	9-7/8

Throw Bed Covers (51cm drop, 5cm double hems allowed): Metric

Bed	Finished Size	90cm	#L	115cm	#L	140cm	#L	150cm	#L	180cm	#L	230cm	#L	300cm	#L	Approx. Trim Meas.**
T	200W x 280L	9.1	3	6.1	2	6.1	2	6.1	2	6.1*	2	3	1	3	1	7.8
D	244W x 300L	9.4	3	9.4	3	9.4*	2	6.2	2	6.2	2	6.2	2	3.2	1	8.5
Q	260W x 300L	9.4	3	9.4	3	6.4	3	6.4	2	6.4	2	6.4	2	3.2	1	8.7
K	304W x 300L	12.7	4	9.4	3	9.4	2	9.4*	3	6.4	2	6.4	2	6.4*	2	9

Comforters (14" drop, 3"-thick batting): Imperial

Bed	Finished Size	36"	#L	45"	#L	54"	#L	60"	#L	72"	#L	90"	#L	120"	#L	Flat Sheets
T	70W x 90L	8-1/2	3	5-2/3	2	5-2/3	2	5-2/3	1	5-2/3*	2	2-7/8	1	2-7/8	1	1 Double
D	85W x 96L	9	3	9	3	6	2	6	2	6	2	6*	2	2-7/8	1	1 King
Q	90W x 96L	9	3	9	3	6	2	6	2	6	2	6	2	2-7/8	1	1 King
K	108W x 96L	12	4	9	3	9	3	6*	2	6*	2	6	2	2-7/8	1	1 King***

Comforters (36cm drop, 7.5cm-thick batting): Metric

Bed	Finished Size	90cm	#L	115cm	#L	140cm	#L	150cm	#L	180cm	#L	230cm	#L	300cm	#L	Flat Sheets
T	180W x 230L	7.8	3	5.2	2	5.2	2	5.2	1	5.2*	2	2.65	1	2.65	1	1 Double
D	215W x 244L	8.25	3	8.25	3	5.5	2	5.5	2	5.5	2	5.5*	2	2.65	1	1 King
Q	230W x 244L	8.25	3	8.25	3	5.5	2	5.5	2	5.5	2	5.5	2	2.65	1	1 King
K	275W x 244L	11	4	8.25	3	8.25	3	5.5*	2	5.5*	2	5.5	2	2.65	1	1 King***

Bed Skirt (Three-sided, 2:1 ruffle ratio, 2" double hems allowed): Imperial

Bed	Finished Size	36"	#S	45"	#S	54"	#S	60"	#S	72"	#S	90"	#S	120"	#S	Flat Sheets
T	14D x 378L	5-1/2	11	4-1/2	9	4	8	3-1/2	7	3	6	2-1/2	5	2	4	1 Twin
D	14D x 428L	6	12	5	10	4	8	4	8	3	6	2-1/2	5	2	4	1 Double
Q	14D x 440L	6-1/2	13	5	10	4-1/2	9	4	8	3-1/2	7	2-1/2	5	2	4	1 Double
K	14D x 476L	7	14	5-1/2	11	4-1/2	9	4	8	3-1/2	7	3	6	2	4	1 Queen

Bed Skirt (Three-sided, 2:1 ruffle ratio, 5cm double hems allowed): Metric

Bed	Finished Size	90cm	#L	115cm	#L	140cm	#S	150cm	#S	180cm	#S	230cm	#S	300cm	#S	Flat Sheets
T	36D x 960L	5		3.7	2	3.7	2	1.8	2	1.8	2	1.8	1	1.85	4	1 Twin
D	36D x 1087L	5.5		4.2	2	4.2	2	4.2	2	4.2	2	2.1	1	1.85	4	1 Twin
Q	36D x 1118L	5.95		7.2	3	4.8	2	4.8	2	4.8	2	4.8	2	1.85	4	1 Double
K	36D X 1209L	6.4		5.8	2	5.8	2	5.8	2	5.8	2	2.9	1	2.9	4	1 Twin

T = twin, D = double or full, Q = queen, K = king   #S = the number of bed-skirt ruffle strips
Important! See notes at the bottom of page 84.
* You may choose to make a slightly narrower cover to economize on fabric—decrease by one length.
** Use this three-sided hem measurement—sides and lower width—when buying or making trims.
***Project dimensions were decreased slightly to accommodate using a king-size sheet, rather than piecing two smaller sheets. If you prefer, substitute two queen-sized sheets and piece lengthwise—see page 77.

Bed Covers: Quick Yardage Calculations

Note: Refer to "Best-Bet Bed Covers," pages 31 – 38.

- *Measure the length and width of the bed.*

- *Determine the desired drop.* Measure for utmost accuracy. The following are guidelines:

  Throws—20" – 21" (51 – 53cm)
  Comforters—14" (36cm) or 2/3 of the top-to-floor drop.

- *Determine if the print requires matching*—see page 81. If so, you will need to add one print repeat to the length calculation (see Step 1, below).

Note: If the comforter has 3" (7.5cm)-thick batting, or more, then add for take-up allowances (see Steps 1 and 2, below).

1. Calculate total length required: Add

Bed length (A)   ____

Drop (C)   +____

Pillow tuck-in allowance (throws only)   +____

18" (46cm) or as desired

Hem/seam allowances—   +____

   8" (20cm) for throws
   1" (2.5cm) for comforters

Length take-up allowance—   +____

   12" (30cm) for twin or double
   13" (33cm) for queen or king

Optional: One print repeat

Total length required   =____

2. Calculate total width required: Add

Bed width (B)   ____

Drop times two (C X 2)   +____

Seam allowances—   +____

   1" (2.5cm) for each seam
   —if uncertain, add 3" (5cm)

Hem allowances—   +____

   8" (20cm) for throws
   1" (2.5cm) for comforters

Width take-up allowance—   +____

   12" (30cm) for twin or double
   13" (33cm) for queen or king

Total width required   =____

3. Calculate number of fabric lengths required:

Total width required—see page 81   ____

Divided by the usable fabric width   =____

Rounded up to the next whole number   =____

Total number of fabric lengths required =____

4. Calculate total inches (cms) required:

Total number of lengths   ____

Multiplied by the total length required   =____

Total inches (centimeters) required   =____

5. Calculate total yards (meters) required:

The total inches (centimeters)   ____

Divided by 36" (100cm)   =____

Total yards (meters) required   =____

More Bed-Cover Yardage & Tips

- *For lofty comforters:* Pin-fit the top and lining over the batting and try on the bed—take-up allowances are not exact. Trim the top and lining length and width as necessary to fit the batting and bed.

- *For the "Remarkable Reversible Quilt"*—see page 35: Add an additional 1/2" (1.3cm) for every 9" (23cm) in width required.

- *For one plain, queen- or king-sized sham, length cut parallel to crosswise grain*—other sizes on page 36:

  1-1/8 yards (1 meter) of 45" (115cm)- or 54" – 60" (140 cm – 150cm)-width fabric.

- *For custom calculating bed-skirt yardage*—see pages 37 and 86. Add 6" (15cm) to the depth from the mattress base to the floor, for hems and fudge factor, and multiply by the number of strips required—see the chart, page 86.

Slipcovers & Cushions: Yardage Estimates for Popular Shapes and Sizes

Drawstring Cushion Covers** (plain top, 2:1 ratio shirred sides): Imperial

Cushion Size	36"	#S	45"	#S	54"	#S	60"	#S	72"	#L	90"	#S	120"	#S	Flat Sheets
22W x 22L x 4D	2	5	1-3/4	4	1-3/4	4	1-1/2	4	1-1/2*	4	1-1/4	2	1-1/4	2	1 Twin

Drawstring Cushion Covers** (plain top, 2:1 ratio shirred sides): Metric

Cushion Size	90cm	#S	115cm	#L	140cm	#L	150cm	#L	180cm	#L	230cm	#L	300cm	#L	Flat Sheets
56W x 56L x 10D	1.85	5	3	2	3	2	1.5	1	1.5	1	1.5	1	1.5	1	1 Twin

Throw Slipcover (2" hems allowed, includes drawstring cushion covers): Imperial   Flat Sheets

Size	#Cushions	36"	45"	54"***	60"	72"	90"	120"***	Throw/Cushion(s)
Easy Chair	1	—	—	7	7	7	7*	5	1 King/1 Twin
Loveseat	2	—	—	9	9	9	9*	6	2 Double/1 Twin
Med. Sofa	3	—	—	12	12	11-1/4	11-1/4*	7	2 Double/1 Double
Med. Sofa	6	—	—	13-3/4	13-3/4	13-3/4	13-3/4*	8	2 Queen/2 Double
Large sofa	4	—	—	14-1/2	14-1/2	14-1/2	14-1/2*	9	2Queen/1 King

Throw Slipcover (5cm hems allowed, includes drawstring cushion covers): Metric Flat Sheets

Size	#Cushions	90cm	115cm	140cm****	150cm	180cm	230cm	300cm***	Throw/Cushion(s)
Easy Chair	1	—	—	6.4	6.4	6.4	6.4*	4.6	1 King/1 Twin
Loveseat	2	—	—	8.25	8.25	8.25	8.25*	5.5	2 Double/1 Twin
Med. Sofa	3	—	—	11	11	10.3	10.3*	6.4	2 Double/1 Double
Med. Sofa	6	—	—	12.6	12.6	12.6	12.6*	7.35	2 Queen/2 Double
Large sofa	4	—	—	13.3	13.3	13.3	13.3*	8.25	2 Queen/1 King

Chair Covers (for 18"W x 16"L x 3"D seats, and 18"W x 20"H x 2"D backs): Imperial

Project	36"	45"	54"	60"	72"	90"	120"	Flat Sheets
Four seats	3	3	1-1/2	1-1/2	1-1/2	1-1/2	3/4	1 Twin
Six seats	4-1/2	4-1/2	2-1/4	2-1/4	2-1/4	1-1/2	1-1/2	1 Twin
Four backs	5-1/2	2-3/4	2-3/4	2-3/4	2-1/4	1-1/2	1-1/2	1 Twin
Six backs	8	4	4	4	3	2-1/4	2-1/4	1 Double

Chair Covers (for 46cmW x 41cmL x 7.5cmD seats, and 46cmW x 51cmH x 5cmD backs): Metric

Project	90cm	115cm	140cm	150cm	180cm	230cm	300cm	Flat Sheets
Four seats	2.75	2.75	1.4	1.4	1.4	1.4	.7	1 Twin
Six seats	4.15	4.15	2.1	2.1	2.1	1.4	1.4	1 Twin
Four backs	5	2.55	2.55	2.55	2.1	1.4	1.4	1 Double
Six backs	7.35	3.7	3.7	3.7	2.75	2.1	2.1	1 Double

Yardages are estimated for solid colors only. Additional yardages will be required for matching large-motif prints. All requirements are based on project length running parallel to the fabric or sheet length; cut crosswise if desirable and necessary to economize—see page 81. Consider cutting the project crosswise, particularly if using sheets or wide-width fabric.

Furniture sizes: easy chair—30"L x 38"H (76cmL x 96cmH), loveseat—60"L x 30"H (150cmL x 76cmH), medium sofa—80"L x 30"H (203cmL x 76cmH), and large sofa—98"L x 30"H (249cmL x 76cmH).

#S= the number of cushion-side strips.

— = no yardages are given for these fabric widths because their relatively narrow width would necessitate too much piecing.

*You may choose to decrease by one length or cut on the crosswise grain to economize on fabric.

**"Gift-wrapped" cushion covers—see page 44—require approximately the same yardage per cushion.

*** You may need to narrow the hem allowance slightly to fit this fabric width.

Slipcovers & Cushions: Quick Yardage Calculations

Note: Refer to "Easiest Slipcovers Ever," pages 39 – 44.

Drawstring Cushion Covers

• *Measure the cushion length, width, and depth.*

1. Calculate total top length required: **Add**

Cushion-top length (A)	_____
Seam allowances—1" (2.5cm)	+_____
Total top length required	=_____

2. Calculate total top width required: Add

Cushion-top width (B)	_____
Seam allowances—1" (2.5cm)	+_____
Total top width required	=_____

3. Calculate total depth required: **Add**

Cushion-cover depth (C)	_____
Seam and casing allowance—2" (5cm)	+_____
Total depth required	=_____

4. Calculate the cover/side perimeter: **Add**

Cushion perimeter	_____
Multiplied by 2 (fullness factor)	=_____
Seam allowances—2" (10cm)+_____	
Total cover/side perimeter required	=_____

5. Calculate total number of side strips required:

Total cover/side perimeter	_____
Divided by the fabric width	=_____
Rounded up to the next whole number	=_____
Total number of side strips required	=_____

6. Calculate total cushion/side inches (cms) required:

Total depth	_____
Multiplied by the total no. of side strips	=_____
Total cushion/side inches (cms) required	=_____

7. Calculate total inches (cms) required: **Add**

Total cushion length or width— whichever will parallel the lengthwise grain.	_____
Total cushion side inches (cms) required	+_____
Total inches (centimeters) required	=_____

8. Calculate total yards (meters) required:

The total inches (centimeters)	_____
Divided by 36" (100cm)	=_____
Total yards (meters) required	=_____

• *For multiple cushions, multiply the total yardage by the number of cushions.*

• *If you want the tops to be identical, cushion to cushion, allow an additional print repeat for each cushion.* Plot the layout strategy before purchasing, or at the least, before cutting out.

Throw Slipcovers

Note: Remove all separate cushions before measuring.

1. Calculate total length: **Add**

FG ____ + GH ____ + HI ____ + IJ ____	_____
Multiplied by 2	=_____
Hem allowances—4" (10cm)	=_____
—40" (102cm) for puddled hems	
Total length required	=_____

2. Calculate total depth: **Add**

AB ____ + BC ____ + CD ____ + DE ____	_____
Hem allowances—4" (10cm)	+_____
—20" – 40" (51cm – 102cm) for puddled hems	
Seam allowances—1" (2.5cm)	+_____
Total depth required	=_____

Note: The fabric must be at least as wide as AB. For piecing options, see page 41.

3. Calculate the yards (meters) required:

Total length required	_____
Divided by 36" (100cm)	=_____
Total yards (meters) required	=_____

If total depth is wider than the fabric width, multiply the total yardage for one length times 2 for the total yards (meters) required. Also, add the total cushion yards/meters (see Step 8, above) to calculate total project yards/meters.

Fabricing:
Yardage Estimates for Popular Applications

Quik Trak® Applications (3" handling ease, plus 6" extra-length allowed): Imperial

Wall/Area	36"	#P	45"	#P	54"	#P	60"	#P	72"	#P	90"	#P	120"	#P	Flat Sheets
48W x 96L	5-7/8	2	5-7/8	2	2-7/8	1	2-7/8	1	2-7/8	1	2-7/8	1	2-7/8	1	1 Twin
72W x 96L	8-3/4*	3	5-7/8	2	5-7/8	2	5-7/8	2	5-7/8*	2	2-7/8	1	2-7/8	1	1 Double
96W x 96L	8-3/4	3	8-3/4	3	5-7/8	2	5-7/8	2	5-7/8	2	5-7/8*	2	2-7/8	1	1 King
120W x 96L	11-2/3	4	8-3/4	3	8-3/4	3	8-3/4*	3	5-7/8	2	5-7/8	2	5-7/8*	2	2 Twin

Quik Trak® Applications (7.5cm handling ease, plus 15cm extra-length allowed): Metric

Wall/Area	90cm	#P	115cm	#P	140cm	#P	150cm	#P	180cm	#P	230cm	#P	300cm	#P	Flat Sheets
218W x 244L	5.4	2	5.4	2	2.65	1	2.65	1	2.65	1	2.65	1	2.65	1	1 Twin
180W x 244L	8*	3	5.4	2	5.4	2	5.4	2	5.4*	2	2.65	1	2.65	1	1 Double
244W x 244L	8	3	8	3	5.4	2	5.4	2	5.4	2	5.4*	2	2.65	1	1 King
300W x 244L	10.7	4	8	3	8	3	8*	3	5.4	2	5.4	2	5.4*	2	2 Twin

Stapled Applications** (3" handling ease, plus 6" extra-length allowed): Imperial

Wall/Area	36"	#P	45"	#P	54"	#P	60"	#P	72"	#P	90"	#P	120"	#P	Flat Sheets
48W x 96L	5-7/8	2	5-7/8	2	2-7/8	1	2-7/8	1	2-7/8	1	2-7/8	1	2-7/8	1	1 Twin
72W x 96L	8-3/4*	3	5-7/8	2	5-7/8	2	5-7/8	2	5-7/8*	2	2-7/8	1	2-7/8	1	1 Double
96W x 96L	8-3/4	3	8-3/4	3	5-7/8*	2	5-7/8	2	5-7/8	2	5-7/8*	2	2-7/8	1	1 Queen
120W x 96L	11-2/3	4	8-3/4	3	8-3/4*	3	8-3/4*	3	5-7/8	2	5-7/8	2	5-7/8*	2	2 Twin

Stapled Applications** (7.5cm handling ease, plus 15cm extra-length allowed): Metric

Wall/Area	90cm	#P	115cm	#P	140cm	#P	150cm	#P	180cm	#P	230cm	#P	300cm	#P	Flat Sheets
218W x 244L	5.4	2	5.4	2	2.65	1	2.65	1	2.65	1	2.65	1	2.65	1	1 Twin
180W x 244L	8*	3	5.4	2	5.4	2	5.4	2	5.4*	2	2.65	1	2.65	1	1 Double
244W x 244L	8	3	8	3	5.4*	2	5.4	2	5.4	2	5.4*	2	2.65	1	1 Queen
300W x 244L	10.7	4	8	3	8*	3	8*	3	5.4	2	5.4	2	5.4*	2	2 Twin

Shirred Applications (2:1 fullness ratio, 6" top/lower casing allowance): Imperial

Wall/Area	36"	#P	45"	#P	54"	#P	60"	#P	72"	#P	90"	#P	120"	#P	Flat Sheets
48W x 96L	8-1/2	3	8-1/2	3	6	2	6	2	6	2	6*	2	3	1	1 King
72W x 96L	11-1/2	4	11-1/2	4	8-1/2	3	8-1/2	3	6	2	6	2	6*	2	1 Queen
96W x 96L	17	6	14-1/2	5	11-1/2	4	11-1/2	4	8-1/2	3	8-1/2*	3	6	2	1 Queen, 1 King
120W x 96L	20	7	17	6	14-1/2	5	11-1/2	4	11-1/2	4	8-1/2	3	6	2	3 Queen*

Shirred Applications (15cm top/lower casing allowances): Metric

Wall/Area	90cm	#P	115cm	#P	140cm	#P	150cm	#P	180cm	#P	230cm	#P	300cm	#P	Flat Sheets
218W x 244L	7.8	3	7.8	2	5.5	2	5.5	2	5.5	2	5.5*	2	2.75	1	1 Twin
180W x 244L	10.5	4	10.5	4	7.8	3	7.8	3	5.5	2	5.5	2	5.5*	2	1 Queen
244W x 244L	15.5	6	13.2	5	10.5	4	10.5	4	7.8	3	7.8*	3	5.5	2	1 Queen, 1 King
300W x 244L	18.2	7	15.5	6	13.2	5	10.5	4	10.5	4	7.8	3	5.5	2	3 Queen*

Yardages are estimated for solid colors only. Additional yardages will be required for matching large-motif prints.
All requirements are based on project length running parallel to the fabric or sheet length; cut crosswise if desirable and necessary to economize—see page 81. Consider cutting the project crosswise, particularly if using sheets or wide-width fabric.

*You may choose to make a slightly narrower panel to economize—decrease by one length or sheet.
**Use stapled-application yardages for starched applications, too—see page 56.

Fabricing: Quick Yardage Calculations

Note: Refer to "Fast Fabricing," pages 51 – 56.

● ***Measure the height and width of wall/area that will be covered with fabric.*** Do not subtract for doors or windows.

● ***Determine if the print requires matching***—see page 81. If so, you will need to add one print repeat to the length calculation (see Step 1, below).

Quik Trak® or Stapled Applications

1. Calculate total panel length: **Add**

Height of area or wall (A)   —––

Handling ease/hem allowances—   +—––

   3" (7.5cm) if stapling
   3" (7.5cm) if using *Quik Trak*®
   6" (15cm) extra-length insurance   +—––

Optional: One print repeat   +—––

Total panel length required   =—––

---

2. Calculate total width: **Add**

Width of the area or wall (B)   —––

   —add additional walls/areas   +—––

Total width required   =—––

3. Calculate the number of panels required:

The total width   —––

Divided by the usable width—see page 81   =—––

   —If stapling, the usable width should allow at least 1/2" (1.3cm) along each lengthwise edge for seaming. If not, subtract 1" (2.5cm) from the usable width.

   — If using *Quik Trak*®, the usable width should allow 1-1/2" along each lengthwise edge for inserting into the track. If not, subtract 3" (7.5cm) from the usable width.

Rounded up to the next whole number   =—––

Total number of panels required   =—––

---

4. Calculate total inches (cms) required:

The total panel length   —––

Multiplied by the total number of panels   =—––

Total inches (cms) required   =—––

---

5. Calculate total yards (meters) required:

The total inches (centimeters)   —––

Divided by 36" (100cm)   =—––

Total yards required   =—––

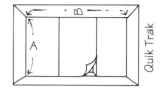
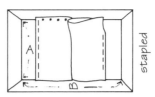
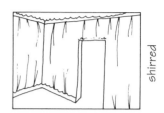

Note: Also look for Easy Home Decorating with Quik Trak®, *a handy how-to and yardage guide—see Quik Trak*®, *page 94.*

Shirred Applications

1. Calculate total panel length: **Add**

Height of wall or area (A)   —––

Add casing/header allowances—   +—––

   6" (15cm) for two (top/lower)
   3" (8cm) for one (only the top)

Total panel length required   =—––

---

2. Calculate total width required:

Width of the area or wall (B)   —––

   —add additional walls/areas

Multiplied by the fullness factor—   =—––

   2 for mid-weights
   2-1/2 for extra fullness
   3 for light-weights

Total width required   =—––

---

3. Calculate the number of panels required:

The total width   —––

Divided by the fabric width   =—––

Rounded up to the next whole number   =—––

Total number of panels required   =—––

---

4. Calculate total inches (cms) required:

The total panel length   —––

Multiplied by the total number of panels   =—––

Total inches (centimeters) required   =—––

---

5. Calculate total yards (meters) required:

The total inches (centimeters)   —––

Divided by 36" (100cm)   =—––

Total yards required   =—––

Photography Credits

Ask for these lines at your local fabric/craft store or department. Showing a picture from this book or my descriptions here should help in your search. If unable to find the specific products shown, you should be able to find a perfectly suitable substitute. Also, see "Sources" on pages 93–95. Enjoy shopping!

Note: Wholesale accounts can write me for company addresses, c/o Open Chain Publishing, Inc., P.O. Box 2634-B, Menlo Park, CA 94026.

Front Cover:

Fabric Traditions, "Jewel Box"; Hollywood Trim, "Continental Collection Cord Edge"; E. E. Schenck, "Antique Scallop" shade frame; Repcon, "Infinity Ring"; HTC "Trans-Web Tape™."

How-to page numbers: table toppings—8, 9 (with satin cord-edge); chair—44; lampshade—61 (with cord-edge trim); curtain—19; trim—75.

Back Cover:

Lower row, left: Concord House, "Polished Apple—English Garden and Geraniums"; Hollywood Trim, "Chair Tie" (napkin tie); YLI, "Woolly Nylon" thread (for all serged finishing).

How-to page numbers: self-lined runner—13 (40" [101cm] extra length was allowed for two end knots); tablecloth—9; napkin—14 (also see "Tassel a cord").

Upper row, center: Concord House, "Polished Apple—English Garden and Pansies" (border was used for tiebacks); Graber, "Double Curtain Rod"; Pellon®, "Thermo-Lam® Plus"; Coats, "Transparent Nylon" thread.

How-to page numbers: curtains (lined in stripe) and tiebacks—16, 17, 71 (interfaced with fleece).

Center row, right: Concord House, "Westbury Gardens" and "Beacon Hill"; Pellon®, "Wonder Shade™"; Hollywood Trims, "Cotton Club Cord-Edge," "La Belle Tassels," "Ragg Mopp Cut Fringe"; Kirsch, Continental® I rod.

How-to page numbers: shade—22, 23 (large tassel was created by wrapping two tassels with fringe and gluing); window scarf—28, 29 (full fabric width was lined with contrasting print, the ends tapered); sleeved rod—30.

Upper row, right: VIP Fabrics, "Rainbow Jungle"; Fairfield Processing, "Poly-fil® Extra-Loft® Batting" and "Soft Touch" pillow form; Dritz, "Craf-T-Fleece™."

How-to page numbers: comforter—32; sheetcase—33; shams and cases—36; knotted pillow—50; sheets—38, 77, 81.

Upper row, left: Concord House, "Beacon Hill"; Repcon, "Frame Decor"; Art Wire Works, shade frame; Quik Trak®, "Quik Trak®"; HTC, "Fuse-A-Shade™."

How-to page numbers: frame—six yards (5.5 meters) each of 13" (33cm)-wide strips in two colors were used alternately, with three loops formed for top bow and excess for streamers (also see pages 66 and 94); lampshade—60; shirred walls—52, 53, or 55.

Center row, left: Concord House, "Beacon Hill"; Repcon, "Infinity Ring"; Hollywood Trim, "Chintz Covered Welting" and "Continental Collection Tassels"; The Cutting Edge, "Success®" thread; Dritz "Fusible Craf-T-Fleece™"; Fairfield Processing, "Soft Touch®"; Mountain Mist, "Pillow-Loft®."

How-to page numbers: slipcover—40, 41 (made toddler-size for photo); stool cover—44; rosette pillow—50; tie-on pillow—50 (upside-down tassels were pushed into center).

Lower row, right: VIP Fabrics, "Christmas"; Repcon, "Wreath Decor" and "Fan Decor"; Hollywood Trim, "Christmas Collection Satin Cord and Tassels" and "Ballerina Tassels"; Madeira, "Glamour™" thread; YLI, "Candlelight™" thread; Pellon®, "Decor-Bond®."

How-to page numbers: ornaments and packages—64, 65, 66 (cord ends were inserted in brass bells); fan/wreath—66 (small "paperized fabric" fans were tied with cord, and taped to form fan shape; round napkins—see page 14—were pulled through every other Wreath Decor ladder for wreath); reversible wired-edge accents—58, 59.

Other Helpful Books by Gail Brown

Ask for other titles by Gail Brown where you found this book. Even if they aren't in stock, all can be special-ordered. Still unable to buy the books locally, or through special or mail order? Open Chain (P.O. Box 2634–B, Menlo Park, CA 94026) welcomes orders (and wholesale inquiries).

Quick Napkin Creations. Packed with the newest tips, gift and decorating ideas, and yardage charts. No-sew, easy-sew, and serged how-to's, plus 18 folds. (Book: $15 postpaid, $16 for CA residents, video: $17.50 postpaid, $18.70 for CA residents.)

Innovative Serging. All-new tips for zippers, collars, flatlocking, piping, couching, fishing line, bead strands, and much more. One-of-a-kind serger-buying guide, plus detailed references/sources.

Innovative Sewing. Newest, fastest how-to's for knits, tailoring, flattering slacks, real leather, *Ultraleather*®, and embellishments. Also, an interfacing update, and finding time and space to sew.

For *Innovative Serging* or *Innovative Sewing*, $16.95 each title postpaid, $18 for CA residents, from Open Chain, address above.

Sources

When looking for decorator fabrics and findings, shop your local stores, in person, and/or by phone (a great way to save gas and time). Take advantage of the service, advice, and first-hand review of prospective colors and textures. However, in case you can't find what you need in area stores, I've compiled this mail-order list. Also, consult **Designer Source Listing, Volume V**, by Maryanne Burgess, ©1992, Carikean Publishing, P.O. Box 11771, Chicago, IL 60611-0771 (800/344-2199) (available for $19.95 postpaid) and the mail-order ads in national sewing publications. Let me know if I've missed your favorites or included a source whose service is questionable. (Reading this more than a year after publication? Send a LSASE to Open Chain Publishing, Inc., P.O. Box 2634-B, Menlo Park, CA 94026, for a free update.)

Note: "LSASE" means a long, self-addressed, stamped business envelope.

Fabrics, Notions, How-to's

Aardvark Adventures, P.O. Box 2449, Livermore, CA 94551. Rayon and other decorative threads, assorted notions, and lots of fun. Catalog/newspaper, $2 (refundable with first order).

Baer Fabrics, 515 E. Market St., Louisville, KY 40202 (800/788-2237, 502/583-5521). 85,000 square feet of fabrics and notions galore. Call for mail-order and swatch-set details, plus extensive notions catalog.

Bemidji Woolen Mills, P.O. Box 277, Bemidji, MN 56601 (218/751-5166). Wool and fiberfill battings. Brochure, LSASE.

BMI Home Decorating, 2237 Bonhaven Rd., Lexington, KY 40515 (800/999-2091). Discounted name-brand fabrics and wallcoverings. Write for free information.

Britex Fabrics, 146 Geary, San Francisco, CA 94108 (415/392-2910). The West Coast's largest selection of designer-quality fabrics. Personalized swatch service, $5.

Buffalo Batt & Felt Corp., 3307 Walden Ave., Depew, NY 14043 (716/683-4100, ext. 8). Batting and forms. Brochure and samples, $1 (refundable).

Calico Basket, 410 Main St., Edmonds, WA 98020 (206/774-6446). Lampshade frames and over 3000 pure-cotton fabrics. Monthly swatched sets available. LSASE for information.

Calico Corners. Call 1-800-821-7700, ext. 810, for the retail outlet nearest you. Large selection of fabrics and accessories, affordably priced.

C.B. Enterprises, 26002-B Marguerite Parkway, Suite 412, Mission Viejo, CA 92692. Source for Repcon products: *Infinity Rings*, *Fan Decor, Frame Decor, Wreath Decor*, and more. Send LSASE.

The Claesson Company, Rte. One, Cape Neddick, ME 03902 (207/363-5059). Contact about "Swagholder" video, $17 (postpaid) and dealer referrals.

Clotilde, Inc., Box 22312., Ft. Lauderdale, FL 33315-2312 (800/772-2891). Special machine feet, *Perfect Pleater*, threads, fusible-transfer web, glues, and much more. Free color catalog.

Cottons, Etc., 228 Genessee St., Oneida, NY 13421 (315/363-6834). Cotton and cotton-blend fabrics. A LSASE (with two stamps) for their list and swatches.

The Crowning Touch, 2410 Glory C Rd., Medford, OR 97501 (503/772-8430). Makers of the *Fasturn* ® turning tool and *Fastube*™ sewing foot, hi/low adaptor. LSASE.

The Cutting Edge., Box 397, St. Peters, MO 63376. Serger threads—all-purpose and decorative, related notions, and books. Catalog, $1 (refundable with order).

Daisy Kingdom, 134 N.W. 8th, Dept. Deco–8, Portland, OR 97209 (800/234-6688, 503/222-9033–ext. 4). Decorating fabrics, kits, books, and supplies, including lampshade frames. Color catalog, $1.

Designer Touches, Inc., P.O. Box 767612, Roswell, GA 30076-7612. Quick-to-make *Window Crowns by Beverly* cornice kits. Send LSASE for information.

The Fabric Center, 488 Electric Ave., P.O. 8212, Fitchburg, MA 01420-8212 (508/343-4402). Offers discounts on most major decorator fabrics. Free brochure.

Fabric Editions, Ltd., Honey Hill Farm, 25 Kenwood Circle #4, Franklin, MA 02038 (800/242-5684). Discounted fabrics for crafts, quilting, and country decorating. "Wholesale Club," and "Yours for a Year" sample program. Color catalog, $3.

Fabrics by Phone Ltd., P.O. Box 309, Walnut Bottom, PA 17266 (800/233-7012). Discount prices on decorator fabric. Know the manufacturer, pattern number, or name and color before you call.

Field's Fabrics by Mail, 1695-44th St. S.E., Grand Rapids, MI 49508 (800/67ULTRA or 616/455-4570). Wide assortment of fabrics, including *Ultrasuede*®.

Fit for You, 781 Golden Prados Dr., Diamond Bar, CA 91795 (714/861-5021). Assorted, hard-to-find notions. Brochure, LSASE.

G Street Fabrics Mail Order Service, 12240 Wilkins Ave., Rockville, MD 20852 (orders, 800/333-9191, fax orders, 301/231-9155). Extensive fabric and book offerings. Notion list, free. Custom samples, $5.

Global Village Imports, 1101 SW Washington, #140, Portland, OR 97205-2313 (phone/fax, 503/274-8778). Guatemalan hand-woven ikat fabrics. Swatched product information, $3.50 (refundable with first order).

Grands, P.O. Box 45, Magalia, CA 95954. "Quick Change Decorating" video (VHS), featuring Repcon products. $14.95 postpaid.

A Great Notion Sewing Supply Ltd., 13847—17A Ave., White Rock, B.C., Canada V4A 7H4 (604/538-2829). Hard-to-find sewing supplies. Catalog, US $1.

The Green Pepper, 3918 West First Ave., Eugene, OR 97402 (503/345-6665) Recreational fabrics, battings, hardware, and zippers. Catalog, $2.

Hancock Fabrics, 3841 Hinkleville Rd., Paducah, KY 42001 (800/626-2723, ext. 456, orders only). Quilting, drapery, and upholstery specialist. Send LSASE for product and fabric listings.

Herrschners, Hoover Rd., Stevens Point, WI 54492 (800/441-0838). Sewing notions, books, and fabrics. Free color catalog.

Home-Sew, Bethlehem, PA 18018. Sewing notions, trims, and basic fabrics, affordably priced. Free catalog.

Homespun 10' Wide Fabrics & Draperies, P.O. Box 3223, Ventura, CA 93006. Heavily textured fabrics, all 120" wide. Catalog and swatches, $2.

Iron-On Drapery Tapes, P.O. Box 8696, Young America, MN 55551-8696. Send $9.95 for the Dritz® 15-minute video, "Making Window Shades & Drapes the No-Sew Way."

Jack's Upholstery & Caning Supply, 5498 Rte. 34, Oswego, IL 60543 (708/554-1045). Hard-to-find upholstery supplies. Catalog, $2.

Keepsake Quilting, Dover Street, P.O. Box 1459, Meredith, NH 03253. Hundreds of 100% cotton calico prints. Free catalog.

Kreinik Manufacturing Co., Inc., P.O. Box 1258, Dept.-Consumer Division, Parkersburg, WV 26101 (800/537-2166). Decorative threads. *Threads & Treasures* needlework-supply catalog. LSASE for free samples.

The Lamp Shop, P.O. Box 36, Concord, NH 03301. Send LSASE for lampshade-frame/accessories information.

Larkshades & Lighting, 20820 Broadway, Sonoma, CA 95476 (707/935-6315). Lampshade findings and frames. LSASE.

Laura Ashley, 1300 MacArthur Blvd., Mahwah, NJ 07430 (800/223-6917 for store referrals). Catalog, $3.

London Fabrics, 2438W. Anderson Lane, Austin, TX 78757 (800/955-3699). Sturdy, easy-to-assemble padded headboard kits. Call for free brochure.

Lois Ericson, P.O. Box 5222, Salem OR 97304. Cloth pleater and neat books. LSASE.

Madeira Marketing, Ltd., 600 East Ninth St., Michigan City, IN 46360 (219/873-1000). Intriguing decorative threads—from metallics and sequins, to neons and rayons. $30 minimum. LSASE.

Mary Jo's Cloth Shop, 401 Cox Rd., Gastonia, NC 28054 (800/MARYJOS). Fabrics, books, and notions. Call with your specific request.

Mary's Productions, P.O. Box 87, Aurora, MN 55705 (218/229-2804) Delightful embellishment ideas. Brochure, LSASE.

Mill End Store, Box 82098, Portland, OR 97282-0098 (503/236-1234). Wide selection of decorator fabrics, notions, trims, threads, and accessories. Inquiry, LSASE.

Nancy's Notions, Ltd., P.O. Box 683, Beaver Dam, WI 53916-9976 (800/833-0690). Wide-width decorator fabrics, plus decorative threads, glues, fusible-transfer web, and machine accessories. Also, ask about their video catalog and club. Free color catalog.

National Thread & Supply, 695 Red Oak Rd., Stockbridge, GA 30281 (800/847-1001, ext. 1688, 404/389-9115). Name-brand sewing supplies and notions. Free catalog.

Newark Dressmaker Supply, P.O. Box 2448, Lehigh Valley, PA 18001 (215/837-7500). Pleating and shirring tapes, decorator fabrics, sewing notions, decorative threads, labels, trims, and laces. Free catalog.

Northwest Sewing, P.O. Box 25826, Seattle, WA 98115 (800/745-5739). Free decorative-thread catalog.

Oregon Tailor Supply, P.O. Box 42284, Portland, OR 97242 (800/678-2457). Notions by the score—excellent prices on coned thread. LSASE.

Outdoor Wilderness Fabrics, 16195 Latah Drive, Nampa, ID 83651 (208/466-1602). "Wilderness" outdoor fabrics and findings. For a complete product/price listing, send LSASE.

Pacific Fabrics Shop at Home, P.O. Box C3637, Seattle, WA 98124 (800/446-6710). Lampshade-frames, fabrics, notions. Swatched "Quilt Shop at Home" color card, $5 (refundable).

The Paris Connection, 4314 Irene Drive, Erie, PA 16510. Full line of sewing, quilting, and craft supplies, machine manuals and accessories. Catalog, $3.

Pierre Deux, 147 Palmer Ave., Mamaroneck, NY 10543. Lovely French-inspired prints and accessories. Write for their retail-store list.

Pine River Textiles, 10443A–124 St., Edmonton, Alberta, Canada T5N 1R7. Outdoor fabrics and more. Catalog, US $2.50.

Quik Trak®, 84 Reservoir Park Dr., Rockland, MA 02370 (800/872-8725). Contact for dealer referrals and books by *Quik Trak®* expert Ann Thomassen.

The Ribbon Outlet, Inc., (800/766-BOWS). Discounted ribbons, trims, crafts, and decor accessories. Call for the store location nearest you.

S & B Sewing Notions, 185 Gordon Rd., Willowdale, Ontario, Canada M2P 1E7. Notions, quilting supplies, books, Catalog, US $2.

Salmagundi Farms, 3185 South State Hwy. 525, Coupeville, WA 98239. Lampshade findings, LSASE.

Sarah's Sewing Supplies, 7267 Mobile Hwy., Pensacola, FL 32526 (904/944-2960). Sewing notions and books. LSASE.

Seattle Fabrics, 3876 Bridge Way North, Seattle, WA 98103 (206/632-6022). *Sunbrella®, Textilene®,* and more. Price list and swatches, $2.

Sew /Fit Co., P.O. Box 565, La Grange, IL 60525 (708/579-3252). Notions, cutting tools, and mats. Free color catalog.

Shama Imports, P.O. Box 2900, Farmington Hills, MI 48333 (313/478-7740). Hand-embroidered wool crewelwork fabrics. Free catalog and swatches.

Solo Slide Fasteners, Inc., P.O. Box 528, Stoughton, MA 02072 (800/343-9670). Notions, books, and zippers in every length and type imaginable. LSASE.

Specialty Fabric Clubs, P.O. Box 586, South Plainfield, NJ 07080 (customer service, 908/755-6171). Request complimentary membership information.

Speed Stitch, 3113-D Broadpoint Dr., Harbor Heights, FL 33983 (800/874-4115). Rayon threads and other machine-art supplies. Color catalog, $3 (refundable with order).

Stitches 'N Stuff, Rte. 2, Box 224, Elmore City, OK 73035 (405/788-4478 or 405/527-2636). *Fab-Lam* fabric-lamination material. Write (LSASE) or call for more information.

Treadleart, 25834 Narbonne Ave., Lomita, CA 90717 (800/327-4222). Sewing/quilting books, patterns, notions, machine accessories, plus bimonthly color magazine. Catalog, $3.

Unique Creations, 28 Cherokee Drive, Newark, DE 19713. LSASE for lampshade-frame details.

Wamsutta/Pacific, 1285 Ave. of Americas, New York, NY 10019. Send $4.95 for *Surroundings,* c/o P.O. Box 774, New York, NY 10108 or order the *Decorating with Sheets* video for $29.95 by calling 800/888-4078. Call 800/344-2142 for store referrals.

Warm & Natural, Cotton batting. Call 800/234-WARM for retail referrals.

Warm Products, Inc., 16120 Woodinville-Redmond Rd., #5, Woodinville, WA 98072 (800/234-9276). Window insulation fabrics/systems. Write or call for dealer referrals.

Westpoint Pepperell, 1185 Ave. of Americas, New York, NY 10036 (800/533-8229 for retail-store referrals). *Decorating with Sheets* booklet, free. Also, how-to videos.

YLI, P.O. Box 109, Provo, UT 84603 (800/854-1932). Incredible threads, yarns, and ribbons, for all-purpose or decorative sewing and serging. Color catalog, $1.50.

Need Help?

Ask your local merchant about custom services and decorating classes. Also:

American Home Sewing and Craft Association, 1375 Broadway, New York, NY 10018 (1-800-U-SEW-NOW). Call for referrals to local sewing courses.

American Sewing Guild, P.O. Box 8476, Medford, OR 97504 (503)772-4059. Network with others who love fabrics, sewing, quilting, and crafts.

Canadian Home Sewing & Sewing Needlecraft Association, 224 Merton St., Ste. 203, Toronto, Ontario, Canada M4S 1A1. Inquire about consumer programs.

The Creative Machine, P.O. Box 2634-B, Menlo Park, CA 94026. Talk to the authors and authorities who are in-the-know. Subscription to this quarterly magazine, $12.

National 4-H Council, 7100 Connecticut Ave., Chevy Chase, MD 20815-4999. (Call your county extension office for local 4-H information.)

Professional Association of Custom Clothiers (PACC), 1375 Broadway, New York, NY 10018 (201/302-2150). National trade association for professionals in sewing-related businesses.

The Sewing Fashion Council, P.O. Box 431M, Madison Square Station, New York, NY 10010. "Home Styling" and "Sewing for the Home" brochures, $2 each postpaid.

Index

Single copies of this book can be ordered from Open Chain Publishing, Inc., PO Box 2634-B, Menlo Park, CA 94026.

Wholesale orders are welcome. Please contact Chilton Book Company, Radnor, PA 19089, (800) 695-1214.